MW01625213

AIRBORNE RANGERS

Alan M. and Frieda W. Landau

BARNES & NOBLE
BOOKS
NEW YORK

Barnett William Landau
1905–1953

This edition published by Barnes & Noble, Inc., by arrangement with MBI Publishing Company

1999 Barnes & Noble Books

M 10 9 8 7 6 5 4 3 2 1

ISBN 0-7607-1648-X

First published in 1992 by MBI Publishing Company

Library of Congress Cataloging-in-Publication Data Available

On the front cover: Rangers board a Black Hawk.

On the frontispiece: By the time a soldier earns the Ranger tab, he is an expert at rappelling down even the slipperiest of cliff faces.

On the title page: Student Rangers learn the art of laying an ambush.

On the back cover: Left, Ranger students jump from a C-130 at dusk to start a field training exercise. Right, Rangers practice assault by water. Bottom, a Ranger instructor teaches a lesson on patrolling.

Printed in Hong Kong

Contents

Acknowledgments

We would like to thank the following, without whose cooperation and goodwill this book would not have been possible.

Col. David Grange, commander, 75th Ranger Regiment, and his staff; Sgt. First Class Ronald Hilston, Regimental S-5; Capt. Joe Stanjones and S. Sgt. Robert Gallagher, 3rd Ranger Battalion S-5; and the Rangers of the 75th.

Col. John J. Maher, commander, Ranger Training Brigade; Lt. Col. Brian M. Pentecost, deputy commander; Maj. Bernie Champoux, executive officer; Command Sgt. Maj. Frederick E. Weekley; and the staff of brigade headquarters.

Lt. Col. Clyde M. Newman, commander, 4th Ranger Training Battalion; Command Sgt. Maj. Donald E. Purdy; and the officers and men of the 4th Ranger Training Battalion.

Lt. Col. Jack Donovan, commander, 5th Ranger Training Battalion; Command Sgt. Maj. Luis C. Palacios; and the officers and men of the 5th Ranger Training Battalion.

Lt. Col. Paul J. Burton, commander, 6th Ranger Training Battalion; Command Sgt. Maj. Velda E. Welch; and the officers and men of the 6th Ranger Training Battalion.

Lt. Col. Barry E. Willey, commander, 7th Ranger Training Battalion; Command Sgt. Maj. Francisco G. Magana; and the officers and men of the 7th Ranger Training Battalion.

Lt. Col. Alexander Angelle, public affairs officer, and Griff Godwin, public affairs specialist, Fort Benning, Georgia.

Capt. Douglas Kinneard, public affairs, Hurlburt Field, Florida.

Z. Frank Hanner, curator, National Infantry Museum, Fort Benning, and his staff.

The staff of the Donovan Technical Library, Infantry Hall, Fort Benning; in particular Mrs. Geneva Brown and Mrs. Betty Van Sickle.

Minolta Corporation for the loan of camera equipment to supplement our own.

Col. Robert I. Channon, US Army (retired).

Mr. Philip B. Piazza, president, Merrill's Marauders Association.

Mr. Tom Walsh and Mr. Les Enekes of the London International Air Show, London, Ontario, for allowing us to interview pilots at their show about special operations support.

Lt. Comdr. Dave Parsons, US Navy.

And finally we wish to thank Marshall LeFavor, who patiently read the rough drafts.

Any errors are ours.

Except where noted, all photographs are by the authors.

Introduction

When Gen. Norman D. Cota urged the small group of Rangers from the 5th Ranger Battalion to "lead the way" off Omaha Beach, Pfc. Ellis E. Reed was chosen to take a bangalore torpedo to blow the concertina wire beyond the seawall. All he had to do was get over the seawall under fire, run up to the wire, and blow it up. It would be just like a training exercise, he was told. And, just as in a training exercise, Private Reed gave the safety warning of "fire in the hole" before he blew a path through the wire large enough for the thirty-five Rangers with him to reach the road above the beach.

Today's Rangers would say that Private Reed was "hooah"—he had the Ranger spirit, a combination of confidence, competence, and enthusiasm. The first question asked of a new member of a Ranger unit, whether in the Training Brigade or the Regiment, is if he is hooah. Will the new member fit into the Ranger community, which is so dependent on teamwork? Will he understand that being a Ranger is an attitude, a state of mind, as well as a matter of skills and training? For that is the most important part.

Rangers know they have received the most arduous and exacting training in the infantry. Their skills have been honed under conditions that come as close to combat as possible. This gives them the confidence to eagerly undertake any task with the conviction that they will succeed. They also know that the other members of their unit will back them up at all times. They are all Rangers, they are hooah!

The term "ranger" or "raunger" is found in England as early as 1455, according to the *Oxford English Dictionary* describing one who is "a forest officer, a gameskeeper." In the North American colonies, it was defined as "a body of mounted troops, or other armed men, employed in ranging over a tract of country." Colonies had a defensive screen of forts and block houses that could never be totally effective against infiltrating Indians. The solution was the employment of small mobile forces that ranged or patrolled the frontier.

In chapter 1 of this book, we have attempted to present a brief history of those units which performed Ranger missions, even if they were not called Rangers. Ranger missions are special light infantry military operations such as strike operations, usually deep penetration, including raids, interdictions, and recovery. Rangers may also do reconnaissance and security missions such as taking and holding an enemy airfield for use by US forces. Thus, Col. Benjamin Grierson's command is included, but some Confederate Ranger units are not. Due to the limited nature of this book, not all Ranger units operating in colonial and early national period America are mentioned.

Chapters 2 and 3 cover the Ranger Training Brigade and the 75th Ranger Regiment, respectively. We have tried to convey an idea of present-day Ranger life and training in these sections.

Anyone wishing to learn more about the history of the Rangers in the United States should consult the works listed in the bibliography.

RANGERS LEAD THE WAY!

Chapter 1

History of the Rangers

Colonial Rangers

"I cannot conceive how war can be made in such a country," wrote a British soldier from America (Beattie 1986). The territories controlled by the British colonists, larger than the mother country, were a trackless and almost uninhabited wilderness. Many of the areas' Indian inhabitants were hostile. Armies operating in America had to operate over large distances, and commanders had to control and coordinate units over these distances. Reinforcements, some supplies, and orders had to come from England, 3,000 miles away.

The British Army recognized these problems before Gen. Edward Braddock's Army met disaster in 1755. George Washington's unsuccessful campaign in 1754 necessitated building a road through what was described as "an immense uninhabited Wilderness overgrown everywhere with trees," so that "no where can anyone see twenty yards" (Gipson 1946-1947). Where roads existed they were "either Rocky or full of Boggs, we are obliged to blow the Rocks and lay Bridges every Day" (Gipson 1946-1947).

When Braddock brought his army to the colonies, they were not unfamiliar with wilderness operations. In Europe and Scotland in the 1740s, commanders experienced wilderness combat, and occasionally conducted operations against guerrillas. Braddock formed nine companies of Virginia troops, of which six were known as Rangers, and a company of light horse Rangers. Similar companies from Maryland and North Carolina were formed, but few of these men were woodsmen, most coming from the tidewater settlements. The general still hoped to employ them "to cover the Main Body of the Army, and shelter it from all Manner of Surprise" (Nichols 1947).

Braddock realized his army might be attacked by irregulars. He trained his troops in march security, created a second grenadier company in each battalion, and lightened the equipment each soldier carried. He bent his efforts toward securing provincial backwoodsmen and Indians for the expedition, but too few Indians enlisted. Even so, "these troops remain so constantly on guard, always marching in battle formation, that all the efforts that our detachments put forth against them are useless," according to French descriptions of Braddock's careful movements before his defeat, just short of his objective, Fort Duquense (near Pittsburgh, Pennsylvania), in a battle that remains controversial (Gipson 1946-1947).

The British turned immediately to the colonists, who used Rangers all along the frontier, reinforced by defensive screens of forts and block houses, between which mobile units "ranged" or patrolled the frontier. Along the southern frontier during King George's War, defections among England's Indian allies led to the building of forts and Ranger patrols in 1746. Gorham's Rangers, active in Nova Scotia since 1750, were an example of what Rangers could do. Gorham, whose unit served the crown until 1765, was the only American Ranger to be offered a regular commission. Gorham's father had also led a Ranger company in Nova Scotia from 1744 to 1750. The British, in 1755, started recruiting frontiersmen from New York and New Hampshire.

One of those recruited was Robert Rogers, a backwoodsman from New Hampshire. Most of the Rangers from western New Hampshire and Massachusetts were to engage in scouting. As auxiliaries of the regular army, they took the Oath to Fidelity, and were subject to the Rules and Articles of War. In 1756 Rogers took command of four companies. Rogers' area of operations was the Champlain Hudson River Valley chain of rivers and lakes, whose strategic value was that they led into either French Canada or New York. These waterways were crucial to the movement of the army, its supplies, and raiders. Since these routes froze in winter, major military operations ceased as armies went into winter quarters. While their most important mission was reconnaissance, during the winter the Rangers could patrol and harass their enemies as well.

Tensions always existed between the Rangers and the regular army. In 1756 Lord Loudoun, commanding the British Army in America wrote, "It is impossible for an Army to Act in this Country, without *Rangers*; and there ought to be a considerable body of them" (Beattie 1986). Later he was less enthusiastic. Rangers proved to be more expensive than regular infantry, and it was often said they were difficult to handle; and in the case of Rogers' Rangers, that only he could control them. Others went further, claiming they were overly fond of rum, going out on patrol only when they felt like it. Regular army officers claimed Rangers would riot when exposed to military discipline. Despite these complaints more Rangers were recruited for the campaign of 1758. By 1757, Loudoun feared that even Ranger intelligence was inaccurate, and began to search for an alternative.

The army could not do without these irregulars, and they remained with the army throughout the Seven Years' War. A process began at this time to train regular officers and trusted men "to beat the woods, & act as *Irregulars*" (Beattie 1986), and to initiate a long-term commitment to develop light infantry capable of wilderness fighting. None of this, though, could be accomplished without the help of the Rangers. While Loudoun determined to convert two companies into Rangers, with the

Standing Orders, Rogers' Rangers

1. Don't forget nothing.
2. Have your musket clean as a whistle, hatchet scoured, sixty rounds powder and ball, and be ready to march at a minute's warning.
3. When you're on the march, act the way you would if you was sneaking up on a deer. See the enemy first.
4. Tell the truth about what you see and what you do. There is an army depending on us for correct information. You can lie all you please when you tell other folks about the Rangers, but don't never lie to a Ranger or officer.
5. Don't never take a chance you don't have to.
6. When we're on the march we march single file, far enough apart so one shot can't go through two men.
7. If we strike swamps, or soft ground, we spread out abreast, so it's hard to track us.
8. When we march, we keep moving till dark, so as to give the enemy the least possible chance at us.
9. When we camp, half the party stays awake while the other half sleeps.
10. If we take prisoners, we keep 'em separate till we have had time to examine them, so they can't cook up a story between 'em.
11. Don't ever march home the same way. Take a different route so you won't be ambushed.
12. No matter whether we travel in big parties or little ones, each party has to keep a scout 20 yards ahead, 20 yards on each flank, and 20 yards in the rear so the main body can't be surprised and wiped out.
13. Every night you'll be told where to meet if surrounded by a superior force.
14. Don't sit down to eat without posting sentries.
15. Don't sleep beyond dawn. Dawn's when the French and Indians attack.
16. Don't cross a river by a regular ford.
17. If somebody's trailing you, make a circle, come back onto your own tracks, and ambush the folks that aim to ambush you.
18. Don't stand up when the enemy's coming against you. Kneel down, lie down, hide behind a tree.
19. Let the enemy come till he's almost close enough to touch. Then let him have it and jump out and finish him up with your hatchet.

MAJ Robert Rogers

Col. William O. Darby, first commander of modern US Rangers. US Army

possibility of forming a separate corps, it was necessary that these "Gentlemen Volunteers" accompany the Rangers on various missions to learn the art of "ranging." Two months later the men were ordered back to their regular units.

Lt. Col. Thomas Gage offered to raise a corps of 500 light armed foot soldiers, recruited from the colonists, with the mobility of Rangers but subject to all regulations. The first of these units was activated on the New York frontier in 1758. Rogers recorded that regulars arrived "to be trained in the ranging or wood-service." Instruction was to include "our methods of marching, retreating, and bushing, fighting, etc., that they might be better qualified for any future service against the enemy we had to contend with" (Russell 1978). Between 1757 and 1758 volunteers went on patrols with Rogers and his men. The light infantry battalion raised in England during this period had many commissioned and noncommissioned officers who had trained with the Rangers.

Lord Howe was instructed by Rogers. Observers noted that Howe made the 55th Foot in the image of the Rangers, but with traditional red uniforms. Howe ordered tails cut off coats and queues off hats, added leggings for protection in the underbrush, and ordered barrels of muskets browned to reduce reflections. By February 1759 one tenth of each battalion of regular troops was formed into a light infantry corps. Gen. Sir Jeffrey Amherst ordered light infantry armed with carbines in place of muskets, and wanted them to "swing pack"—move out—at a moment's notice, so they could move swiftly through the wilderness. In addition, they displayed discipline and staying power.

The Rangers were helping to change the tactics of the British Army in the wilderness. Every regiment was trained to skirmish, patrol, and move quickly through the forests. Regular troops were soon carrying thirty pounds of meal which they cooked. Some discarded knapsacks and, in Ranger fashion, carried a blanket roll. In 1756 some British units instructed their men in the art of firing and loading while prone or kneeling. In June 1758 ten rifles were issued in each battalion to arm the best marksmen. Movement was facilitated by discarding some equipment and training each man to move in order "slow and fast in all sorts of Ground" (Beattie 1986).

Despite these changes the regulars still needed Rangers. In 1757, Loudoun determined the army needed increased winter scouting, so he sent home many provincials raised in the northern colonies and asked these same colonies to furnish a contingent of 1,100 experienced Rangers. Rogers saw that his Rangers were specially equipped for winter scouting. Each man had a haversack for dried food and spare flints and a canteen made of wood, or tin, that carried about two quarts of a mixture of rum and water. A blanket roll was draped over one shoulder with its ends tied together at the opposite waist. Weapons consisted of a tomahawk, a scalping knife, and a musket, usually sawed down for better handling in the field, with sixty rounds of ball and powder, often supplemented by buckshot. Some carried bayonets.

During cold weather, mittens were attached to sleeves or carried around the neck on strings. Snowshoes were carried on the back when not in use. The blanket could also serve as a hood, and those who could afford them wore army capotes or watch coats. Extra supplies could be carried on hand sleighs or toboggans. Travel across frozen lakes and rivers was aided by barbed ice creepers attached to the soles of moccasins and shoes.

On the march, an advance guard was deployed. During the winter they were equipped with ice skates. Use of flankers and reconnaissance parties was standard at all times, though mistakes were made. Rest stops and camping at night meant that pickets were set out in all directions. Beds of spruce boughs were placed around a fire pit dug to a depth of three feet. The pits minimized the chances of detection by the enemy. At dawn, the usual hour for an attack, the men were drawn into ranks. If the enemy failed to attack, breakfast was taken and the march continued.

Throughout the period from 1758 to 1760, Rogers' Rangers carried out a series of long-range reconnaissance patrols against French positions in the area of Fort Ticonderoga, New York. In March of 1759, Rogers led a force of fifty-two Indians, 169 light infantry, and ninety Rangers to scout Fort Carillon at Ticonderoga. They returned with valuable intelligence, several scalps, prisoners, and a sketch of the fort.

In 1760 Amherst ordered Rogers to move against the Abenaki Indians at St. Frances. He was to take 200 Rangers and to "remember the Barbarities that have been committed by the enemy's Indian scoundrels" (Beattie 1986). The Rangers crossed 200 miles of wild terrain while losing one quarter of their strength to sickness, lameness, and injuries. The Indians were surprised: between 100 and 200 Indians were killed, and the town was burned. Only two of Rogers' men were lost in the attack. While returning, proper discipline was not

Battle flags and colors of the 2nd Ranger Battalion, World War II. US Army

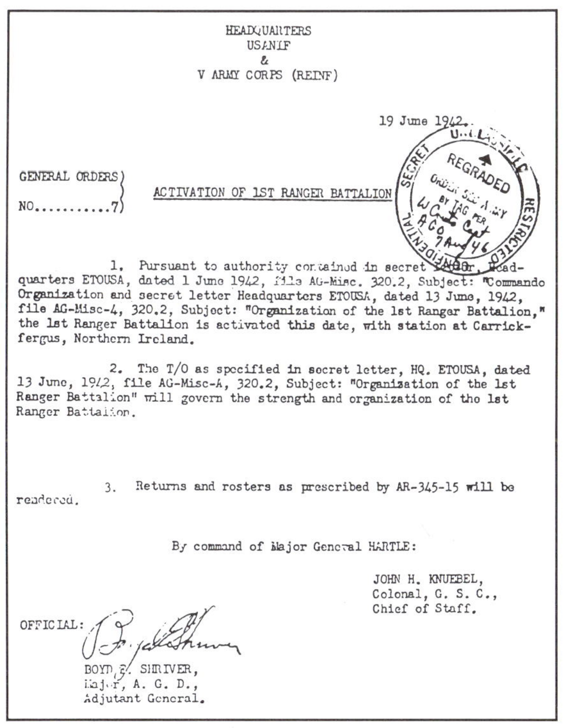

HEADQUARTERS
USANIF
&
V ARMY CORPS (REINF)

19 June 1942.

GENERAL ORDERS
NO..........7

ACTIVATION OF 1ST RANGER BATTALION

SECRET REGRADED UNCLASSIFIED ORDER SEC ARMY BY TAG PER AGO 7 Aug 46 CONFIDENTIAL RESTRICTED

1. Pursuant to authority contained in secret letter, Headquarters ETOUSA, dated 1 June 1942, file AG-Misc. 320.2, Subject: "Commando Organization and secret letter Headquarters ETOUSA, dated 13 June, 1942, file AG-Misc-4, 320.2, Subject: "Organization of the 1st Ranger Battalion," the 1st Ranger Battalion is activated this date, with station at Carrickfergus, Northern Ireland.

2. The T/O as specified in secret letter, HQ. ETOUSA, dated 13 June, 1942, file AG-Misc-A, 320.2, Subject: "Organization of the 1st Ranger Battalion" will govern the strength and organization of the 1st Ranger Battalion.

3. Returns and rosters as prescribed by AR-345-15 will be rendered.

By command of Major General HARTLE:

JOHN H. KNUEBEL,
Colonal, G. S. C.,
Chief of Staff.

OFFICIAL:

BOYD F. SHRIVER,
Major, A. G. D.,
Adjutant General.

Order activating Darby's Rangers.

Shoulder patch of 1st Ranger Battalion, World War II. The current patch of the 75th Ranger Regiment is modeled on this style.

enforced. One third of the men, already hungry and tired, fell prey to "enraged" pursuers or starvation.

By Gen. James Wolfe's Canadian campaign of 1759, the British Army had learned to fight in the harsh terrain of the Americas. As Wolfe's Army moved it was protected by screens of light infantry and Rangers. The general ordered detachments never to halt, encamp, or cross dangerous areas without scouting. All camps and outposts were to be fortified against sudden attacks. If they occurred the retreating force was to use light infantry to screen the withdrawal to draw the enemy into battle with the main army.

Rangers in the Revolution and the Early Republic

Throughout the American Revolution, both sides used light infantry and irregular forces,

Commando knife specially made for Darby's Rangers. The handle of the knife doubles as brass knuckles.

which often took part in the increasingly bitter intercommunal strife between Loyalist Tories and Whig Rebels.

In 1776, George Washington gave Col. Thomas Knowlton permission to form a unit of Rangers that would perform "delicate" and hazardous duty. Formed from about 120 men from New England regiments, the unit was positioned near the East River above Harlem. It reconnoitered in front of American lines and, while operating with Gen. Nathanael Greene's troops, attempted to reach the rear of the British lines to cut off the enemy.

Though the Rangers were adept at moving through difficult terrain, the operation was a failure, and Knowlton was killed. The unit surrendered with the garrison at Fort Washington 16 November 1776.

British Ranger units operated from Canada, infiltrating New York State and Pennsylvania, joining Indian allies in destroying houses, barns, grain, and grist and saw mills. They aimed at interdicting supplies from the Mohawk Valley to the Continental Army.

Gen. Frank D. Merrill (middle). US Army via Phil Piazza

Intercommunal warfare was particularly fierce in the south. From 1780 until war's end, Col. Francis Marion played a substantial role in combating England's southern strategy. British Army planners believed they could drive the Whigs from areas of power by using Loyalist partisans. Slowly, but inevitably, they would pacify each colony, finally restoring colonial government.

Marion's career as a partisan Ranger began in 1780. Without an independent command, and intrigued by the partisan activities of American Gen. Thomas Sumpter, he agreed to direct militia activities near Williamsburg, an area of Whig influence. American Gen. Horatio Gates consented, ordering Marion, in August 1780, to disrupt supplies from Camden to British Gen. Charles Lord Cornwallis.

Marion and his men knew the woods and swamps well and, armed with a variety of weapons, carried out lightning raids against British and Tory forces. They often loaded their muskets with buckshot or musket ball and three or four buckshot. It was not uncommon for partisans to score the musket ball so it would break into fragments, inflicting more damage than ordinary shot.

In the fall of 1780, General Cornwallis wrote that "Col. Marion has so wrought on the minds of the people . . . that there was scarce an Inhabitant between the Santee and the Peedee who was not in

Merrill's Marauders at the start of their mission. Note the contrast to the Marauders as supplies became scarce. US Army via Phil Piazza

arms against us." British Col. Banastre Tarleton, sent to run Marion down, reported that his foe could bring his men together rapidly, and "after making incursions into the friendly districts, or threatening the communications, to avoid persuit, he disbanded his followers" (Scheer 1958). Marion frequently held up supplies sent to the British Army.

Having failed to bring his foe to bay, Tarleton is supposed to have declaimed: "Come on, my boys, let's go back. As for this damned old fox, the devil himself could not catch him" (Scheer 1958). Having eluded Tarleton, Marion continued to raid until his supplies ran low. Moving to a place in the swamps in the Lynch Creek and Great Pee Dee, both in South Carolina, he set up a supply and rest camp. From this base he continued to harass the British and their Tory allies, keeping the "whole country in continual alarm," so that regular troops were "everywhere necessary" (Scheer 1958).

In 1781 Marion joined with Gen. "Light Horse" Harry Lee and invested Fort Watson, South Carolina. They soon joined Gen. Nathanael Greene's troops at Eutaw Springs, South Carolina on 8 September, forming the right wing of Gen. Greene's line. Placed to absorb the first shock of battle, they were to fall back after firing as many rounds as possible. Greene hoped to use Daniel Morgan's successful Cowpens' strategy—having the militia and regulars retreat after firing their initial rounds. After four hours of fierce fighting, each side lost about 500 men, either killed or wounded. Though outnumbered, the British troops broke the first two Continental lines. Not wishing to risk his last unbroken regiments, Greene withdrew. Cornwallis also suffered heavily and moved to Wilmington, but later retreated into Virginia. Greene said Marion's men had a "degree of Spirit and firmness," that "would have graced the soldiers of the King of Prussia [Frederick the Great]" (Ferling 1984).

Greene, who followed Cornwallis north, was soon back in South Carolina where he was joined by Marion and others. Greene was defeated near Camden, South Carolina, but Marion cut the British line of communications at Fort Watson, forcing a British retreat. Marion spent the remainder of the war hunting Tories and trying to keep supplies from reaching British troops in Charleston. In 1782 his brigade was officially disbanded.

East Florida, along the Georgia border, was the scene of constant guerrilla activity. By 1777 the Loyalists in east Florida and nearby Georgia formed the East Florida Rangers. Supplemented by a small body of Creek Indians, their leader, Thomas Brown, carried out a series of raids into Georgia. While some raids were of little military value, they succeeded in bringing cattle and other

Merrill's Marauders crossing a primitive mountain bridge in Burma. The lack of food can be seen clearly in the skeletal appearance of the men. US Army via Phil Piazza

forage into food-poor east Florida. Brown attached his Rangers to Indian war parties to prevent "indiscriminate butchering of women and children" (Olson 1970).

Throughout the war, Brown, the governor of Florida, and the local military authorities argued over the status and rank of the Rangers. The army won, and many of the old Rangers (men of property) did not wish to accept the terms of the new provisional establishment and left the service. At the end of 1779, Brown formed a new corps, the Kings (Carolina) Rangers. They were issued new uniforms consisting of a short green coat with crimson collar and cuffs and plain green lapels. While stationed on the Georgia border, they drove cattle from rebel areas and worked among Loyalists in the back country. At war's end, many moved to Barbados.

Merrill's Marauders receiving a very rare resupply by parachute. Such drops were usually impossible because of climate or terrain. US Army via Phil Piazza

The early national period saw continued unrest along the frontier. Consequently the states, and later the federal government, continued to use Rangers units. In the 1800s, Congress was interested in the immediate protection of the frontier from Indian raids. On 2 January 1812, six companies of Rangers, recruited from the area, were raised for the protection of settlers. Men enlisted for twelve months. They equipped and provided for themselves and their horses at an allowance of one dollar per day. While they brought security to the frontier settlements, the Rangers were not strong enough to assert American rights, as European nations still held territory on the frontier.

In 1814 there were 1,070 Rangers, and ten independent companies, patrolling the frontier from Michigan to Louisiana. In 1818, Gen. Andrew Jackson commanded Ranger units in the Florida panhandle. A mounted Ranger battalion was formed between 1832 and 1833. It was employed to show force against the Indians, especially when bargaining, and for protection of commercial routes. Essentially, it was part of Andrew Jackson's Indian policy. In 1832, the secretary of war, Lewis Cass, reported that the Rangers were merely "superior militia" who were unruly and had difficulty working with regular infantry. Costing $150,000 more than a regular dragoon regiment, they did not receive special training.

Nevertheless, the government decided mounted units were useful, and despite earlier fears that cavalry was an aristocratic threat to democracy, the secretary of the army moved to enact legislation discharging the Rangers, and enlisting dragoons.

Throughout the 1830s, Ranger units were used in Texas. In 1832 they were employed along the frontier and were separate from Texas' regular army and militia. Texas Rangers had no regular uniforms and furnished their own arms. Rangers were used in the Mexican War, despite Zachary Taylor's poor opinion of them; he found them indispensable as scouts. Twenty or more Ranger companies served Texas between the war with Mexico and the Civil War.

The Civil War

It is estimated that some 428 units were officially and unofficially known as Rangers during the Civil War. Their effectiveness has been questioned, and many were Rangers in name only. On 21 April 1862, Confederate President Jefferson Davis approved an act to form partisan Rangers to be organized as infantry or cavalry. Captured military equipment would be considered "booty," as the act declared: "The Rangers shall be paid their full value in such manner as the Secretary of War may prescribe" (Grant 1958).

From the beginning, the units were controversial. Problems arose because they siphoned troops away from regular units and were allowed to profit from confiscated goods. Brig. Gen. Henry Heth, of West Virginia, announced that they were "a terror to the loyal and true everywhere," being no better than robbers and plunderers. He found that they were "more ready to plunder friends than foes . . . they do as they please—go where they please," which meant "roaming over the country, taking what they want, and doing nothing" (Grant 1958).

While some units, such as Mosby's Rangers, had good reputations, disillusionment with their operations was rising. Confederate Secretary of War James A. Seddon believed that the advantages of such units had been only "partially realized," and that their "independent organization and the facilities and temptations thereby afforded to license and depredations grave mischiefs have resulted" (Grant 1958). He concluded that they should be disbanded and the men merged with troops of the line.

In 1864, Gen. Robert E. Lee was informed that "[Rangers] are a terror to the citizens and an infamy to the cause. They never fight; can't be made to fight." Many, he was told, "have engaged in this business for the sake of gain." Lee was

Patches and badges of the Ranger companies in Korea.

Shoulder patches and badges of the Ranger companies in Vietnam. The insignia in the center is the badge of the Vietnam Ranger Association. The shield in the center is the badge of Merrill's Marauders. The motto continues to be the motto of the 75th Ranger Regiment. Sfc. R. Hilston, US Army

convinced and soon recommended that "the law authorizing these partisan corps be abolished" (Grant 1958). This was done, with some exceptions, in February 1864.

Rangers were organized for the Union and were used to counter Confederate Rangers. Their contribution to the war is equally obscure. Col. Benjamin Grierson's two raids into Mississippi, though, are similar to Ranger operations. As Gen. Ulysses S. Grant prepared to move against Vicksburg, he instructed Grierson to move south into Mississippi where he was to destroy as much as possible. Grant hoped Grierson's activities would pull Confederate troops out of Grant's operational area.

From 17 April to 2 May 1863, Grierson's mounted troops rode through parts of Mississippi. Having eluded pursuers, he wrecked more than fifty miles of railroad and destroyed several supply bases. Though Confederate leaders were aware this was a diversion, some troops were pulled away from opposing Grant's operations at Vicksburg. This raid was made famous in the movie *The Horse Soldiers*.

Less well known was Grierson's later, winter raid. In some ways this raid was more successful than the first. Gen. Henry Halleck wanted to cut supply lines to the Army of Tennessee. Once Confederate Gen. John B. Hood had been defeated by Union Gen. George H. Thomas before Nashville, a cavalry attack directed at railroads would destroy the major lines of communication to the defeated Confederates.

Very much like Merrill's Marauders of a later war, Grierson's men marched long distances. They accounted for 600 prisoners and 800 head of captured livestock. Some 1,000 slaves deserted their owners, thus denying their services to the manpower-poor Confederacy. Grierson's men destroyed as much track and rolling stock as possible. Already short of supplies, the Confederacy could ill afford the loss of the warehouses with commissary, quartermaster, and ordnance stores. A total of 5,000 stand of arms and 500 bales of cotton had now been destroyed by Grierson.

World War II

The United States did not deploy Ranger units again until World War II. Early in the war, Gen. George C. Marshall decided to train US troops in commando methods. They would gain experience accompanying the British on raids. Brig. Gen. Lucian Truscott, Jr., and Gen. Dwight D. Eisenhower discussed the planning, organization, and conduct of combined operations, eventually deciding to form a commando-type organization.

Eisenhower did not want to use the term commando, as this was already intimately associated with the British. Truscott chose Rangers because the name had been used by American units that had displayed "high standards of individual courage, determination, ruggedness, fighting ability, and achievement" (King 1981). Officially, they would be identified as the 1st Ranger Battalion. Training began at Carrickfergus, Northern Ireland, in June 1942.

Guidelines for Ranger volunteers were determined, the goal being fully trained soldiers of the highest standard. Officers and noncommissioned officers had to show leadership skills, with particular emphasis on initiative, judgment, and common sense. Selectees needed skills in self-defense, weaponry, scouting, mountaineering, seamanship, and small boat handling. Those with skills in demolition and knowledge of railway engines and public utilities, such as power plants and radio stations, were needed.

Volunteers were trained in speed marches, cliff climbing, obstacle courses, and tactical problems. During training, British commandos simulated enemy resistance by throwing grenades and firing small arms over and near the Rangers. Throughout training, the men worked in pairs—a buddy system. Having chosen partners from their platoons, both men trained and lived together. Teams negotiated the bullet and bayonet course, as well as the obstacle course, together. During movement, one team would cover another, and the street fighting course soon became known as "Me and My Pal."

During the war there were six Ranger battalions. The 1st, 3rd, and 4th fought in the Mediterranean theater. The 2nd and 5th went ashore on D-day, 6 June 1944. The 6th and Merrills Marauders fought against the Japanese. These units were originally designated Ranger battalions, but were redesignated Ranger infantry battalions in August 1943.

The 1st Ranger Infantry Battalion was formed in June of 1942 at Carrickfergus, Northern Ireland, and trained there and elsewhere in England before participating in the landings in North Africa in November 1942. The battalion took part in the invasion of Sicily in July 1943. Following Sicily, the unit landed in Italy at Salerno in September 1943, and was destroyed at Cisterna during the Anzio campaign of January 1944.

First Lieutenant and Staff Sergeant of 2nd Platoon, L Company Rangers, 101st Airborne Division, in Vietnam, 1971. The yellow Ranger tab is on the beret. The airborne insignia is on the left shoulder. US Army via Col. David Grange

The 4th Ranger Infantry Battalion was formed in North Africa in May 1943. The 4th, along with the 1st and 3rd battalions, formed Ranger Force for the landings in Sicily and Italy. The unit suffered fifty percent casualties at Anzio. They continued to fight on into February, and were then used to conduct patrolling school for the Fifth Army.

The 2nd Ranger Infantry Battalion was formed in April 1943 at Camp Forrest, Tennessee. They arrived in England on 29 November 1943, and took part in the D-day landings, assaulting Pointe Du Hoe. They saw action in Brest, and later in the Ardennes-Alsace areas, ending the war in Czechoslovakia.

The 5th Ranger Infantry Battalion also formed at Camp Forrest. They arrived in England on 17 January 1944. The battalion landed in Normandy on D-day. After Normandy, the unit saw action in northern France, the Ardennes-Alsace area, the Rhineland, and central Europe. In April 1945 the unit was tasked by Gen. George Patton to escort 1,000 Germans through the Buchenwald death camp.

The 6th Ranger Infantry Battalion was formed at Hollandia, New Guinea, from the 98th Field Artillery Battalion and saw action in the Philippines. Three days before the first landings in the Philippines, they landed on Dinagat, securing the island. During the landings on Luzon, they landed on White Beach and participated in the drive on Manila. During this time they liberated a prisoner of war camp.

Operation Torch

The 1st Rangers, now under the command of Col. William O. Darby, were scheduled to land at Arzew east of Oran, Algeria, as part of Operation Torch (the invasion of North Africa), in November 1942. They were to reduce the main defenses nearby and capture the port of Arzew. Once this was accomplished, they were to capture and secure the beachhead for further landings. The destruction of the coastal defenses was necessary before the rest of the force could land, for if the Rangers failed, naval gunfire would be necessary, alerting the defenders. The Rangers were successful.

During operations in Tunisia and North Africa, the Rangers were employed in a variety of missions, not always in line with their training. Early in February 1943, Darby led the Rangers on a night raid against Italian front-line positions, killing or wounding about seventy-five Italians, destroying one antitank gun and five machine guns, and capturing eleven prisoners. Ranger casualties included one killed and twenty wounded. Unfortunately, when the Rangers were used as regular infantry, as happened, especially during and after the disaster at Kasserine Pass, Tunisia, their casualties increased.

On 13 March, Gen. George S. Patton ordered Darby to assist in the attack on Gafsa, Tunisia. Finding the town lightly defended, the Rangers passed through to regain contact with the enemy. Once contact was restored, they were to determine the enemy's strength and disposition and maintain themselves in the area of contact, while attempting to identify enemy units.

Information obtained from these operations was vital for Patton's planned attack on Italian forces at El Guettar, Tunisia. Darby was told to act aggressively, but not to commit himself to actions from which he could not withdraw. The Rangers were now ordered to infiltrate enemy lines and attack the Djel Jel Ank Pass from the rear while the 26th Infantry Division attacked from the front. Patrols mapped out a route to the rear of the Italian positions, and Darby personally carried out a daylight reconnaissance against the north wall of the pass. Night reconnaissance continued, enabling the Rangers to map a tortuous ten-mile route to an unguarded rocky plateau overlooking the enemy positions.

As the Rangers overran the Italian positions in the mountains, the 26th Division entered the pass. A little before noon, division operations directed Darby and the infantry to clean up what resistance remained, and take the high ground further on. As the attacks continued toward the east, the Rangers were returned to El Guettar.

Invasion of Sicily

When Patton's 7th Army landed in Sicily on 10 July 1943, the Rangers landed with the lead elements of the invasion forces on the beaches near Gela. The Ranger Force consisted of the 1st, 3rd, and 4th Ranger Infantry Battalions. They captured the town, and defended it against counterattack. Their mission included the destruction or neutralization of the coastal defenses located on high ground northwest of Gela. Once secure in Gela, the

Rangers seized the high ground surrounding the town.

Ranger units also landed with the 3rd Infantry Division on Green Beach, where they destroyed enemy installations before moving to the southwest to seize and hold strategic ground until relieved. From these positions the 3rd Ranger Battalion moved inland. Patton now employed the Rangers in his armed reconnaissance to Porto Empedocle. Ranger units penetrated thickly defended areas. On their approach to the city, they ambushed an Italian motorized company. Many of the enemy were killed and so many prisoners were taken that they had to be sent back to the 7th Army lines. On 17 and 18 July, the Rangers entered the town and moved to take the port, afterward setting up a perimeter defense around the city. Ranger units moved toward Messina, and also participated in taking that city.

Invasion of Italy

Following the fighting in Sicily, the Rangers prepared for the invasion of Italy. When the Allies came ashore, the Rangers participated, landing about twenty miles west of Salerno. Their objective was to capture Salerno and destroy nearby coastal defenses. Moving inland, they seized the Chiunzi Pass and prepared to operate against the rear of the enemy. By midmorning, their mission was accomplished. They soon found themselves involved in regular infantry actions, where they sustained more than seventy men killed or wounded.

Operations in Italy reached a stalemate, and a plan to outflank the Germans was devised. It was hoped that with the Allies landing at Anzio, the Germans would be forced to withdraw northward while keeping out of the Alban Hills. The Rangers were taken out of combat to prepare for the landing.

The extensive combat operations in North Africa and Sicily had resulted in Ranger casualties, and the training received by Ranger replacements was apparently not as complete as for the first volunteers. Evidence of this came on 17 January 1944 during a practice landing west of Naples.

After landing, umpires noted that some units made excessive noise and moved when flares were fired, making them more visible than if they had stayed still. Men of the 1st Ranger Battalion established themselves in indefensible positions and failed to send security forward when necessary. Moving inland the 4th Ranger Battalion traveled up a road in column without an advance

Camp Eagle, Republic of Vietnam, 1971. The Ranger companies in Vietnam deployed out of base camps like this one. Conditions were often little better at camp than out in the field. US Army via Col. David Grange

2nd Platoon, L Company Rangers return to Camp Eagle after an interdiction operation near the Ashah Valley in Vietnam. Not all of the headgear is regulation. US Army via Col. David Grange

guard and moved through a defile without proper reconnaissance. Either of these actions could result in an ambush.

Anzio Landing

In the early morning hours of 22 January 1944 the Allies put Sixth Corps ashore on the beaches of Anzio, Italy. The town lay in the middle of the invasion area, and was secured by Darby and his Rangers. To the east of Anzio, the US 3rd Infantry Division, reinforced by the 504th Parachute Infantry Regiment, landed near Nettuno. To the west of the Rangers in Anzio the British 1st Division came ashore. The beachhead was established, but the Allies were too weak to take advantage of the surprise.

The ranger Force consisted of 1st, 3rd, and 4th Ranger Infantry Battalions with assorted units attached, including the 83rd Chemical Battalion, and a cannon company. The Rangers remained in the front lines until shortly before the planned attack out of the beachhead was to take place.

At 0100 hours on 30 January 1944, the Rangers began their movement toward the town of Cisterna di Lattoria, which they were to seize and hold until relieved, after which they were to occupy the ground to the immediate northwest. The 1st and 3rd Battalions crossed the line of departure first, moving along a ditch that offered some concealment. Third Battalion became lost, and then contact between the two units was broken. Radio contact with Darby at his command post was interrupted as it became obvious German troops and armor had infiltrated in and around the advancing Rangers.

The Rangers had to fight their way to Cisterna and arrived at dawn only to find Cisterna garrisoned. In this situation the plan called for support from the 4th Ranger Battalion, but the battalion's forward movement had been stalled by heavy resistance. Fierce fighting continued throughout the area. For those Rangers still in the Pantano ditch, the fighting was brutal. The Germans drove their tanks to the edge, lowered their guns, and fired.

Carlo D'Este, in his *Fatal Decision*, says some Rangers were "deliberately spared, pulled from the ditch and formed into a ragged column," to shield the Germans as they moved toward American lines. Incoming fire killed several prisoners and a witness reported "the Germans machine-gunned and bayoneted some of the helpless prisoners in the column. They had already shot the wounded men left in the ditch."

Very few survived. Of the 767 men who reached the town, only six made their way back to American lines; the rest were killed or captured.

Despite the failure at Cisterna, the Rangers inflicted 5,500 casualties on the Germans, forcing them to commit their reserves and postpone their attack for two days, giving the Allies time to prepare.

Members of 2nd Platoon, L Company Rangers, extracted after a reconnaissance patrol in Vietnam, 1971. The machine gun in the right background is part of the armament of the UH-1 helicopter that extracted the Rangers. US Army via Col. David Grange

First Special Services Force

Those Rangers who survived either were transferred to training units in the United States or were incorporated into the First Special Services Force (FSSF) which was in the area. The FSSF was an American and Canadian unit developed at the urging of British Prime Minister Winston Churchill. The unit was never used in Norway, as originally planned, but was used in the Aleutians and later in Italy.

Though not usually considered a Ranger unit, its training and operations were in the Ranger tradition. Airborne training was completed in six days as opposed to three weeks. Cold-weather training included skiing, rock climbing, mountain walking, use of ropes, and basic cold-weather survival training.

During the many nights spent in mountains during the winter, basic infantry skills were stressed. Training included marksmanship, small arms and automatic weapons, bazookas, mortars, flamethrowers, demolition training, and the use of captured German weapons. Training was so realistic that bayonet training was done with bare blades.

Training continued near Norfolk, Virginia, where they practiced amphibious landings. Further training continued in Vermont in the use of rubber boats, scouting and patrolling, raiding, and demolitions.

On 15 August 1943, under cover of darkness, the unit landed on the island of Kiska in the Aleutians. The raiders found the island evacuated.

General Eisenhower wanted the FSSF in Italy, where it was assigned to the 5th Army in November of 1944. While in Italy, they participated in several attacks through mountainous terrain. In their assault on Mount de la Difensa on 2 December 1944, the FSSF climbed the face of a sheer cliff believed to be unclimbable. This accomplishment in fog and drizzling rain completely surprised the Germans.

The FSSF continued to operate in this forbidding terrain, often moving through sparsely settled areas in separate columns capitalizing on stealth and night fighting capabilities. On 30 January 1944, the unit was ordered into the Anzio beachhead, where they held a portion of the line. During this time they aggressively patrolled the area to their front so successfully that the Germans were forced to pull back their lines. In the final breakout the FSSF accompanied the US Army to Rome, where it occupied strategic bridges over the Tiber River. Passing through the city, they continued to scout while clearing resistance and posting signs for the main body, thus allowing the 5th Army to move past Rome with some degree of security.

The FSSF's last major operation was to secure two strategically placed islands off the coast of southern France during Operation Anvil, the invasion of southern France. The terrain on both islands was formidable, and landings were made on beaches where the cliffs rose from the sea. The FSSF was disbanded on 5 December 1944.

D-day

On 6 June 1944, the Allies landed on the beaches of Normandy, France. The Rangers landed with the assault troops at Pointe du Hoe, four miles west of Omaha Beach. Here the Allies believed the

The total security force for the Desert One hostage rescue attempt. Company C, 1/75, rehearsed under conditions similar to the actual mission. For a deliberate-response operation such as Desert One or Operation Just Cause (Panama), the Rangers meticulously go over every detail beforehand. For quick-response operations such as Grenada, when there is no time for rehearsals, the Rangers rely on their combat-oriented training for success. US Army via Col. David Grange

Germans had emplaced heavy guns that could fire on the beaches.

Sheer cliffs rose from a narrow strip of beach some 85 to 100ft above sea level. Once on the cliff, the Rangers would be in an area mined and crisscrossed with barbed wire. German supporting positions on the flanks consisted of machine and antiaircraft guns.

To accomplish their mission the Rangers were equipped with specialized equipment. Their landing craft carried rocket launchers at the bow, amidships, and in the stern that could be fired either in series or in pairs from one control point at the stern. The rockets would carry 3/4in ropes and light rope ladders to the top of cliffs. Ropes and ladders had grapnels to secure them to the cliffs. Extension ladders, with Lewis machine guns attached to the top, were also carried.

Rangers carried an assortment of infantry equipment, including two hand grenades, an M-1 rifle, and D-bar rations. Some carried pistols or carbines. Heavier weapons included Browning Automatic Rifles, light mortars, and thermite grenades. After the assault wave, more ammunition and heavy mortars were scheduled to land.

On D-day all did not go as planned. High seas soaked the Rangers and their equipment. They realized at the last minute that they were heading for the wrong beach and had to change direction, delaying their attack. Some of the Germans had recovered from the naval and air bombardment and were ready to oppose the Rangers as they scaled the cliff. The beach contained no cover, although the shell holes produced ready-made foxholes. Some fifteen Rangers became casualties on the beach.

The high seas not only soaked the Rangers but also their equipment. The ropes, saturated with water, were too heavy for the rockets to boost to the cliff above the beach. A hand-held launcher finally succeeded in hauling a rope to the crest. The wet Rangers and their ropes produced slippery mud as they struggled to reach the top, where the defenders fired or threw grenades at them.

Once on top, the Rangers found the area desolate, all landmarks gone. Eventually, assault teams neutralized or destroyed the fortifications. To their surprise, the German howitzers were gone but were found later some distance away and destroyed by thermite grenades. Ranger units that had moved inland were attacked during their first night in France, and eventually pushed back to the cliff above the water. Naval gunfire helped the Rangers maintain their positions, and by D + 2 they were relieved.

As the 2nd Ranger Battalion was delayed getting ashore and had trouble scaling the cliff, the 5th Ranger Battalion landed in the Vierville sector behind the 116th Infantry Regiment. Working their way toward Pointe Du Hoe, together with the engineers, they knocked out strong points flanking Omaha Beach.

Following D-day, the Rangers moved inland. The 2nd Ranger Battalion received replacements during July 1944, and with the 5th Ranger Battalion participated in the fighting for the port city of Brest (August-September 1944). In the assault, the 5th Ranger Battalion destroyed several pill boxes with explosive charges and twenty gallons of petroleum oil, which burned for forty minutes. Many Germans surrendered similar positions the next day.

The 2nd Ranger Battalion moved eastward to the Heurtgen Forest, Germany. In December 1944, they were ordered to move to an area overlooking the Schmidt and Roer dams. The Rangers were used to assault a hill that regular infantry had failed to capture. Despite counterattacks, the Rangers held. They were relieved on 9 March.

Toward the end of the war, the 5th Ranger Battalion was employed in a long-range penetration. On 23 February 1945 they were relieved from duty with the 3rd Cavalry Division and given a new mission. They were to pass through the division bridgehead and infiltrate enemy lines, finally establishing a blocking position across the Irsch-Zerf road in Germany.

Several small engagements were fought on the way to the objective. Some Germans were captured, and the objective cleared of enemy troops. The Rangers set up a perimeter that included antipersonnel mines. When the Germans realized the potential of the blocking position, they attacked. Despite orders to fight to the last man, many Germans surrendered. The mission lasted longer than expected; attempts were made

The battle at the Commendancia, Gen. Manuel Noriega's headquarters in Panama City. This was the fiercest fighting in the city during Operation Just Cause. US Army

to supply the Rangers from the air, but gunfire kept the aircraft at 1,500ft and the supplies landed outside of the perimeter. Friendly armor reached the Rangers on 26 February and passed on through the block. The final action was an ambush of German troops in enveloping fog. The Rangers killed an estimated 299 enemy soldiers, taking 328 prisoners, during an operation lasting five days. Afterward, the Rangers were used as regular infantry, a role for which they were not suited.

Philippines Invasion

In the Philippines, the 6th Ranger Battalion took part in preinvasion landings on strategically located islands, guarding the entrance to Leyte Gulf. Going ashore on 17 October 1944, three days before main units landed, they destroyed radio facilities and anything else of military value.

With US forces storming into the islands, the US high command was concerned that the Japanese would move prisoners from the camp at Cabanatuan. The camp was located behind enemy lines, in the mainstream of enemy troop movements, and was a resting place for retreating troops. The main road in the area was used by Japanese trucks and tanks.

A plan was developed to send the Rangers behind enemy lines, free the prisoners, and move them safely back to American lines. The route passed through heavily forested areas, open grasslands, and rice paddies. The Rangers crossed the Talavera River at midnight, and later that night crossed the Rizal road. Guerrillas gave support in the form of intelligence and established a roadblock on the main road. Despite the long route to the objective, and the presence of Japanese forces on the road, the Rangers arrived safely at the camp. Their attack was a surprise. Having freed the prisoners, they now had to escort them to safety. This part of the mission was completed when the group reached a patrol of the 6th Army.

Merrill's Marauders

At the Quebec conference (August 1943), the United States agreed to form a long-range-penetration unit, similar to the British Chindits, for use in Burma. On 1 September 1943, the unit's size was fixed at a battalion. The Army wanted at least 300 rugged, physically fit volunteers from the Southwest Pacific. Seven hundred more were required from the South Pacific, and more than 1,000 were taken from the Caribbean Defense Command and Army in the United States. Among the volunteers were veterans of Guadalcanal, New Guinea, and other Pacific battlegrounds.

These men were brought together under the command of Gen. Frank D. Merrill and were popularly known as Merrill's Marauders. After arriving in India they began training in the tactics of long-range penetration. Locations for jungle training were chosen; but in several of them, conditions, particularly sanitation, were bad. This training lasted for slightly more than two months during which marksmanship, scouting and patrolling, map reading, jungle navigation, calisthenics, and marches with packs were part of the course.

Platoon tactics were stressed, as well as combat team and battalion level movements. Rifle platoon leaders and NCOs were trained to direct mortar fire, and all were taught the rudiments of voice radio. In general, heavy weapons, intelligence, reconnaissance, pioneer, demolition, and communications specialists were already trained, but were further hardened by training with the group.

Rear echelon units included parachute riggers and so-called kick-out units whose job was to deliver supplies to the unit from aircraft. These units prepared adequate supplies in advance so they were ready when the long-range patrols needed them. The pilots were carefully trained, especially for low-level drops into small clearings. All of this was made more difficult by poor flying conditions over Burma.

Facilities were set up for supplies, and arrangements made for radio communication with the units to be supplied. Merrill was in contact with forward units by radio. Long- and short-wave radios were carried in order to coordinate movement of columns and to contact higher headquarters. Long-range radios were carried on mules. Units also carried SCR-300 walkie-talkies with a range of about three miles—a ten-mile range in level terrain, rare in Burma.

On 8 January 1944, the unit, officially known as 5307 Composite Unit (provisional), or Galahad, was assigned to Gen. Joseph Stillwell's command in northern Burma. This was an extremely difficult area in which to operate because it was crisscrossed by rugged hills, high mountains, and deep valleys cut by numerous rivers. A good part of the area was covered by thick jungle, in which strands of bamboo grew so thick that tunnels were cut through them. Troops crossing rivers often emerged covered with leeches. During monsoon season, the area became almost impassable. Mountainsides became so muddy that men and animals slipped and stumbled in the mire, and some areas were so steep that men carved steps in the slopes. Added to this were rain, high humidity, and temperatures producing heat prostration. Mosquitoes and mites carried diseases including common malaria and scrub typhus—and some more exotic.

Galahad was noted for rapid movement and ability to move over what seemed impassable terrain. Its reconnaissance and intelligence platoon always moved ahead of the main body, sometimes by as much as several miles, and one of its rifle platoons formed the first element of the main body. A rifle company with half of the heavy weapons platoon was next in line. The middle of the formation contained the column headquarters, transport, and medical detachment. The rear consisted of a rifle platoon and the rest of the heavy weapons. On occasion, some columns separated the combat elements from support elements so they would not delay the tactical deployment in case of combat.

In the field, the wounded were first treated by medical corpsmen and surgical teams traveling with the unit. Once initial care was given, casualties were removed to the rear by light aircraft which landed on nearby dry riverbeds, rice paddies, and gravel bars along rivers. They were then taken by transports to a hospital equipped to handle them. These aerial ambulances were stationed at Ledo.

On 24 February, Galahad began a series of operations in conjunction with Chinese troops. They were sent on a wide encircling movement east of Chinese forces, where they were to block trails and cut Japanese supply lines when possible. For several weeks the men marched through the jungle, blocking Japanese movements and destroying whatever supplies they could find. Unfortunately, part of Galahad was trapped at Nhphum Ga, where they suffered from combat and disease, and as the official history reports, "The fighting edge of the most mobile and most obedient force that Stillwell had was worn dull" (Romanus 1956). No compensating damage was done to the Japanese, who moved to the defense of Myitkyina airfield, Burma.

The remaining Marauders followed the Japanese to attack Myitkyina airfield. Moving swiftly, they arrived at the field before the enemy realized

The men's room at the Panama City International Airport after a firefight between Rangers and Noriega's forces. This battle encompassed the heaviest fighting at the airport. US Army

they were there. In a quick daylight attack, the field was taken. Stillwell now ordered Galahad to take the town of Myitkyina, a mission for which the unit was not suited and was physically unable to perform.

Galahad now had some 1,000 men out of the original 3,000. Most of their casualties resulted from disease and exhaustion. All were undernourished. One survivor said, "We were perpetually famished" (Ogburn 1959). K-rations lacked bulk and "every fourth or fifth day we ran out of them" (Ogburn 1959). Men would pick up and eat the maltose and dextrose tablets discarded by others. Two conditions existed: "One in which we felt unfed, the other in which we *were* unfed" (Ogburn 1959).

As hunger increased the men engaged in eating rituals which included the precise cutting of a bar of chocolate. Closing one's eyes and "chewing [a cocoa bar] together with [a] soft biscuit gave [the] illusion of eating a chocolate cake" (Ogburn 1959). Unfortunately, after an hour men were once again hungry; and when asleep, hunger returned, as "after midnight [there was] constant waking up to gnawing in belly" (Ogburn 1959).

Having taken the airfield at Myitkyina, the men believed they would be relieved, as they had been promised. Morale plummeted, and Galahad began to lose cohesion. This was compounded when hospitalized men were ordered to return to the front, including many who were not fit for service. In one incident, doctors took sick men off aircraft heading for Myitkyina and sent them back to hospitals. Once relieved and in the rear, discipline was difficult to maintain, and most of the men were unfit for further action.

From the start Galahad seemed doomed. Men from the Pacific already had malaria, other chronic diseases endemic to the area, and psychiatric complaints. Blanket malarial treatment was ordered for all of the 3rd Battalion of Merrill's Marauders. Daily suppressive Atabrine treatment was ordered, but men had to be checked regularly to see that they complied. When morale dropped, this became difficult. Even after periods of rest, the men failed to regain their strength. Improved rations did not help and "the men continued to decrease in strength and endurance and their physical and mental lassitude and exhaustion continued to increase until the very last" (Stone 1969). Doctors reported that "never before has severe exhaustion syndrome been so manifest on such a large scale. . . . Before the third month of combat, evidence of marked adrenal insufficiency began to be noticed in the men" (Stone 1969).

Stillwell's command, and those who failed to see that Galahad could no longer function, were responsible for the unit's deterioration. Merrill stated that promises of relief after three months had been made, and that when asked to move to Myitkyina the men had been told this was the last mission. Unfortunately, Merrill's poor health—he was evacuated twice because of his heart—meant there was no one to fight for the unit at Stillwell's headquarters. The unit was later reconstituted and operated for the rest of the war as Mars, ending the war in China.

At the end of World War II, Ranger units were disbanded. Successful in many of their operations, Rangers were often committed to operations for which they were neither trained nor equipped. In large measure this was because combat troops were scarce, and it was often impossible not to commit the Rangers to battle.

Korean War

Shortly after the end of World War II, the United States and the Soviet Union agreed to partition Korea at the 38th parallel. On 25 June 1950, the North Korean Army attacked across the 38th parallel, pushing deep into South Korea. The United States, with United Nations (UN) support, moved to counter this attack, and American air and ground troops were committed under the command of Gen. Douglas MacArthur. Following MacArthur's brilliant landing at Inchon, South Korea, 15 September 1950, US troops stormed into North Korea, some units reaching the Yalu River, Korea's border with China. Chinese troops entered the war, fighting UN forces to a stalemate, as neither the United States nor its allies desired more than a limited war fought for limited purposes. In the early phases of the war, while the fronts remained fluid, Ranger units were trained and committed to combat in Korea.

Gen. J. Lawton Collins, US Army chief of staff, impressed by the success achieved by infiltrating Communist units at the beginning of the war, sent a memo to Army Operations in Washington, D.C., asking that one company of Rangers be attached to each division, where they would be used to "infiltrate through enemy lines and attack command posts, artillery, tank parks, and key communication centers or facilities" (Lanning 1988).

Eventually, six Ranger companies would be sent to Korea, attached to the 8th Army. Rangers would be attached to the 1st Cavalry, and the 2nd, 3rd, 7th, 24th, and 25th Infantry Divisions, where they would fight in almost all the major battles from their arrival in late 1950 until their deactivation in the fall of 1951.

In the Far East, requests for volunteers were circulated for a unit designated Raiders, but to be known as the 8213 Provisional Company. They were activated in August 1950 and saw action with the 25th Infantry Division until the arrival of the 5th Ranger Company from Fort Benning, Georgia.

Training of Ranger companies began on 2 October 1950 at Fort Benning, Georgia. During this period entire companies trained as units. The original companies were all white, but on 9 October, Fort Benning received a company of black airborne volunteers. Initially designated the 4th Ranger Company, but operating as the 2nd Ranger Company, they were the only all-black Ranger company in US Army history.

The Ranger Training Command was set up at Harmony Church, Fort Benning, where the companies proceeded to pass through the training cycle. The initial cycle lasted six weeks, but the cycle period soon went from a forty-eight-hour week to sixty hours. Training included demolition, sabotage, land navigation, hand-to-hand combat, and communications.

Each training day began with a five-mile run, calisthenics, and long-distance marching with full equipment. The goal was "to prepare a Company to move from forty to fifty miles cross-country in twelve to eighteen hours, depending upon terrain" (Black 1989). Each company was thirty percent overstrength to allow for men who would fall out of the program.

Cold weather training and mountain training were given in a four-week course at Camp Carson, Colorado. Everything was difficult in the mountains of Colorado where the air was thinner and the temperatures low. Equipment issued included special boots for better traction, thermal underwear, fur-lined pile caps, and parkas. Special mittens, called trigger finger mittens, were issued along with shoe packs, rucksacks, and pack boards. Two-man mountain tents with white interiors that allowed the tent to be heated with a candle were used.

In the mountains, men learned how to cross swiftly flowing streams, and to move through draws, ravines, and canyons. Movement through snow and ice was facilitated with ice axes and pitons. Rappelling and snowshoe walking were practiced, along with tactics and techniques previously learned at Fort Benning in better weather.

Cold weather rations included one meal bar, ten cigarettes, one soup packet, and packets of tea, coffee, cream and sugar. These rations were supplemented by extra iron and necessities such as matches and toilet paper. Following mountain and cold weather training, the Rangers were marched to a corral where they were taught to work with mules.

In Korea, Ranger units were used for reconnaissance, sabotage behind enemy lines, and blocking enemy movements. As in previous wars, they were used in operations for which they were not equipped, such as spearheading infantry attacks or holding vulnerable positions of the line.

In March 1951, eleven Rangers were dropped behind enemy lines to blow up a railroad tunnel in the Wonsan area, but failed to do so. They were hampered by deep snow, and Chinese troops were present in large numbers. The Rangers' SCR-300 radios failed to operate until it was too late. Three Rangers were eventually evacuated by helicopters, but the rest were killed or captured. Later in March the Rangers were again used in an airborne operation, Tomahawk, to block enemy troops retreating from the area around Seoul. The operation began on 23 March 1951, with the 2nd and 4th Rangers working with the 187th Airborne Regimental Combat Team. The Rangers seized several

Bedroom of Noriega's beach house, searched by Rangers after the airfield at Rio Hato was secured. US Army

hills and, supported by aircraft and mortars, cleared and captured a village.

These operations are illustrative of the missions carried out by Ranger units in Korea. By the middle of August 1951, the front lines had begun to harden, and pressure mounted to deactivate the Rangers. This process began, officially, on 10 July 1951, when the Department of the Army issued message 95587 directing the inactivation of Ranger companies in Korea. General order 584 was issued on 25 July 1951 declaring that the 1st, 2nd, 3rd, 4th, and 5th, and the unit known as the 8th Army Rangers, were to be inactivated, and that this should occur on 1 August 1951. Those personnel rated and designated as parachutists were to be reassigned to the 187th Airborne Regimental Combat Team which would ensure that the unit would have a full complement of men.

Many forces worked against the Rangers at this time. Many division commanders with attached Ranger units complained about their austere organization, and especially that they could not supply themselves. Some argued that Ranger companies drained desperately needed elite troops from regular units, and that the concentration of superior leaders in a few units was a luxury the Army as a whole could not afford. The final blow to the Rangers in Korea was the static nature of the war in its last years, for units now would have little opportunity to operate successfully behind North Korean and Chinese lines. The argument was advanced that the mostly Caucasian Rangers would find it difficult to operate effectively in areas populated by Asians, an argument that ignored the history of Galahad behind Japanese lines in Burma.

The Ranger training program was to continue, though. Ranger Training Command was inactivated, but immediately reconstituted as the Ranger Department of the Infantry School. This organization would be responsible for training in doctrines, tactics, techniques, and organization. The course would be established so as to provide infantry officers and NCOs assigned to infantry units with training in Ranger operations. The new situation was stated in the last entry of the Diary of Ranger Training Command: "Selected individuals will receive a course of instruction in Ranger tactics and will return to their parent organization to serve as Ranger Instructors therein" (Black 1989).

Vietnam War

At the end of the Korean War no Ranger companies, battalions or regiments existed in the US Army, and this situation continued until the 1970s. In 1969 the Long Range Reconnaissance Patrols (LRRPs)—which had a similar mission and organization but were identified as separate companies and detachments—were designated as Rangers. Pressure to do this was applied by many, including the Merrill's Marauders Association. They felt that the Rangers should have a place in the Vietnam-era Army, and LRRPs were doing Ranger-type operations.

On 16 January 1969, the Department of the Army issued a message designating LRRPs as letter companies of the 75th Infantry Regiment to become effective 1 February 1969. Two new Ranger companies, A at Fort Benning, Georgia, and B at Fort Carson, Colorado, were to be formed. On 7 March 1969, the Department of the Army issued a field manual titled *Long Range Reconnaissance Ranger Company*.

A typical LRRP mission in Vietnam lasted from five to seven days; a mission lasting more than a week was unusual. Missions were limited by human and logistical considerations, for men slept little while in the field, and everything needed was carried on the men's backs.

It was common practice for a team to be assigned a four-square-kilometer zone in which to operate. On the fifth or sixth day of the mission an ambush site was chosen. The team would remain in this position for twenty-four to forty-eight hours. Once an ambush was initiated, they would move immediately to the landing zone (LZ) for extraction.

Each team was composed of six men. This number of men provided enough firepower for security and offensive actions against small enemy units, but they were small enough to move without too much noise, and large enough to divide into two three-man teams. Units this size could conceal themselves along trails, but there would still be enough men to care for the wounded and to continue the fight. Also, larger teams would have needed more than one Huey helicopter for transport.

Planning for each mission lasted two or three days. Before a mission, available intelligence was reviewed. This included maps, aerial photographs, weather and light data, after-action reports, ground and airborne sensor data, agents, and any prisoner interrogations available. LRRPs kept their own files collected from previous missions complete with maps and overlays.

Insertion was accomplished by boats, truck, foot power, and helicopters. On the way in, helicopters might make false approaches to several LZs, or order false artillery barrages. After insertion, units moved in several hundred meters, where they would sit quietly for about an hour, listening. When sure they were not spotted, they would make a quick communications check and then move out on the mission. The time between missions would usually be three to four days for rest and essential planning for the next one.

In 1973, perhaps with the Yom Kippur War in mind, the Pentagon became concerned with the lack of mobility of US Army infantry units. A need was perceived for light infantry which could be moved quickly to any trouble spot in the world. Thus, in January 1974, Gen. Creighton Abrams ordered the formation of Ranger battalions. "This elite unit is to be composed of highly trained and motivated Airborne, Ranger qualified personnel" (Lanning 1978).

On 25 January 1974, the Army ordered the activation of the 1st Battalion (Ranger), 75th Infantry, which would be effective on 31 January 1974, to be stationed at Fort Stewart, Georgia. This was followed on 1 October 1974 by the activation of the 2nd Battalion (Ranger) at Fort Lewis, Washington. Companies A and B were disbanded, since the Rangers would now be doing much more than reconnaissance. The Rangers were now dedicated not only to battlefield missions, but also to "national strategic objectives" (Lanning 1978). The 3rd Battalion (Ranger) would not be activated until after Grenada, on 3 October 1984.

Desert One

The ill-fated attempt to rescue the American Embassy personnel held hostage in Teheran, Iran, code-named Desert One, was primarily a Special Forces operation. It is not generally known that Rangers were also to take part. While 1st Special Forces Operational Detachment—DELTA—was to perform the actual rescue, Company C, 1st Battalion, 75th Ranger Regiment (1/75), was to provide security for the men and equipment.

The rescue force assembled in Egypt on 21 April 1980. Three days later, a fleet of C-141s carried the 120-man force to Masirah Island, off the coast of Oman, where they transferred to three MC-130s accompanied by three fuel-bearing EC-130s. They

Rangers guarded civil aircraft of many countries after securing the Panama City International Airport. The Rangers not only protected the aircraft from harm, but helped prevent false damage claims against the United States by photographing what they were guarding. US Army

landed 200 miles southeast of Teheran at 2200 hours and waited for the arrival of eight RH-53D Sea Stallion helicopters from the aircraft carrier *Nimitz*. A twelve-man road watch team, composed primarily of Rangers, was along to secure the landing site while the helicopters refueled. The team would return to Egypt on one of the MC-130s.

DELTA was to be flown to a hidden shelter (HIDE) site before dawn on 25 April by the RH-53Ds, which would remain at their own HIDE site until the assault on the compound where the hostages were held. The plan was to use the helicopters to ferry the hostages to waiting transport.

The task of Company C, 1/75, was to secure a landing area for the transports. The Rangers were to fly from Egypt to Manzariyeh, Iran, and take the airfield there. They would land, if possible, or jump if resistance was offered. Once the airfield, which was thirty-five miles south of Teheran, was secure, the Rangers would hold it while C-141 StarLifters arrived to airlift the hostages and their rescuers to Egypt. The Rangers would then "dry up," or remove all signs of their presence, render the field useless, and be airlifted out themselves.

Taking and securing a hostile airfield within enemy territory is one of the primary components of the Ranger mission. They were prepared to hold the field as long as necessary if there were not enough transports to take everyone out in one trip. During training, the Rangers worked out all probable scenarios on a mock-up of the type of airfield in Iran.

Desert One was aborted at the first stage when two Sea Stallions crashed into each other on landing, killing their crews. One helicopter had aborted before leaving the carrier. It had been decided that at least six helicopters were necessary for the mission to succeed. Fewer than six automatically cancelled the rescue attempt. Company C, 1/75, never left Egypt. The Rangers in the road watch team returned with DELTA.

Grenada Invasion: Operation Urgent Fury 25-28 October 1983

The Rangers had little time to prepare for their role in Urgent Fury, the invasion of Grenada. Within hours of receiving orders to move, Ranger units were marshalling at Hunter Army Air Field, Alabama, prepared to board C-130s and MC-130s for the ride to Grenada. Their first objective was Salines airfield, located on the island's most southwestern point. While securing the airfield, Rangers were to secure the True Blue Campus at Salines, where American medical students were in residence. As quickly as possible, Ranger units were then to take the army camp at Calivigny.

Things started to go wrong as the operation began. A Navy SEAL team was unable to get ashore; they were to have provided intelligence on the airfield at Salines. H-hour, originally scheduled during darkness, was moved several times until morning twilight. In the lead MC-130s there were problems with the inertial navigation equipment. Since there were no hatch-mount antennas on the cargo doors of the aircraft, communications to Ranger units would be delayed while passing through Air Force communications.

While in the air, the Rangers were notified of photographic intelligence indicating obstructions on the field. Instead of landing, the majority of transport would have to drop all the Rangers at Salines so the runway could be cleared.

In some aircraft the men were told to remove their harness, rucksack and main and reserve parachutes. These items were placed in kit bags and moved forward to facilitate off-loading troops and cargo. Before long, the loadmasters were yelling, "Only thirty minutes fuel left. Rangers are fighting. Jump in twenty minutes."

These Rangers now had to re-rig for the drop, unpacking nonessential equipment and pulling on parachutes. Rucksacks had to be hooked under the reserve pack and weapons strapped to the left side. Under these conditions it was not possible for the jumpmaster to check each man, so buddy rigging was employed.

Aboard the lead MC-130, navigation equipment failed and the pilot reported he could not guarantee finding the landing zone. Rain squalls made it impossible to employ a lead change, so both lead aircraft pulled away to the south. As the Rangers approached the target, the aircraft were out of assigned order and the planned order of arrival was no longer possible. This meant that the runway clearing team would not be the first on the field. The Rangers then requested a mass parachute assault, a contingency previously planned, so that only the order of exit from the aircraft would be affected. But the Air Force would not conduct a mass drop.

At 0534 the first Rangers began dropping at Salines: a platoon of B Company and the Battalion Tactical Operations Center (TOC), followed almost twenty-five minutes later by part of A Company, 1st Battalion, 75th Rangers. Over a half hour later the rest of A Company, 1/75, minus seven men were over Salines. It was now 0634, but the remaining men of the 1/75 would not be on the ground until 0705.

Men of 1/75 assembled on the east end of the runway. They were short C Company, which had been sent with about sixty Special Operations Forces troops to take the Richmond Hill Prison. The Ranger battalions were already operating below strength. One reason for this seems to have been the fact that a limited number of aircraft and aircrews were trained for night operations.

Over one and a half hours elapsed from the first drop of the 1/75 until the last unit was on the ground shortly after seven in the morning. These men jumped from 500ft so they would be in the air between twelve and fifteen seconds. Their drop zone was very narrow because there was water on the north and south sides only a few meters from the runway.

At 0707 the 2nd Battalion (2/75) began to drop. For several hours their aircraft had orbited, waiting to unload and refuel. They dropped in a much shorter period, and all but one man was safely on the ground. One Ranger broke his leg, and one Ranger's static line became tangled as he exited the aircraft, dragging him against the tail of the plane before he was hauled back aboard. The 2/75 assembled on the western end of the runway.

Once on the ground, the 1/75 was not under effective fire, and thus could begin to clear the runway of blocking trucks and bulldozers. Some of the vehicles had keys in them; others were hot-wired and removed. A Cuban bulldozer was used to flatten the stakes that had been driven into the ground with wires between them, and to push aside the drums placed on the runway. For fifteen minutes there was no enemy fire, and the Rangers worked without interruption.

By 1000, A Company, 1/75, had its second platoon at the True Blue Campus and its first and third platoons had moved north of the runway. In the center, B Company, 1/75, had moved north and was holding the high ground not far from the Cuban headquarters. On the left, to the west, units of 2/75 had cleared the area to the west of the airfield as well as the area north of their drop zone to Canoe Bay. The airfield was secure, and the C-130s, which had gone to Barbados to refuel, returned to unload equipment not dropped—which included jeeps, motorcycles, and Hughes 500 Defender helicopters.

Eight hours after landing, the commander of B Company, 2/75, was notified that two Rangers were missing near their positions. The company commander decided the missing men must be near a building which lay between B Company and the Cuban positions. A Cuban construction worker was sent forward with an eleven-man Ranger squad under a flag of truce. While the Rangers remained outside, the Cuban entered and spoke with those inside, who agreed to a truce if the Rangers would treat the Cuban wounded. Two Rangers and seventeen wounded Cubans were evacuated. Afterward, the Ranger commander called for the Cubans to surrender, and eighty to 100 did so. The remainder surrendered later, after a brief fight, to the 82nd Airborne.

At 1530 that afternoon, a counterattack was launched toward A Company, 1/75, consisting of three BTR-60s, which moved through 2nd platoon's positions, firing toward the runway. The Rangers countered with rifles, M60 machine guns, light antitank weapons, and a recoilless rifle. Two of the BTRs hit each other when the first one halted. Both were disabled. The third began a hasty retreat and was hit in the rear. It was finally destroyed by an AC-130 Spectre gunship.

The last action of this first day took place east of True Blue Campus, where Rangers came under fire from a house on top of a prominent hill, 1,000 meters east of the runway. No Spectre gunship was available, so an A-7 attack plane finally destroyed the house, but only after several duds landed alarmingly near the Rangers.

A medical evacuation exercise during preoperational training before Desert Storm. Ranger medics carry weapons. Only the platoon medic receives his medical training before he becomes a Ranger. The squad medics and all team, squad and platoon leaders receive basic emergency medical training from the Regiment. US Army via Col. David Grange

At the end of this first day in Grenada, the Rangers had secured the airfield and True Blue Campus at a cost of five dead and six wounded. Unfortunately, C Company, 1/75, had run into a more difficult situation. When their Black Hawk helicopters arrived at the prison, the local defenses were active. Perched on a high ridge whose sides were almost vertical and covered by dense foliage, the prison was surrounded by walls twenty feet high topped with barbed wire and watchtowers covering the area. Intelligence had failed to report the presence of two antiaircraft guns on a ridge some 150 feet higher than the prison, which brought the Black Hawks under fire. It was impossible to use ropes to lower the Rangers. The helicopters had to remain steady during this operation, making the Rangers and the crews easy targets. No air support was possible at this time, since all aircraft were engaged at Salines.

At least two attempts were made to bring the Black Hawks in to unload the troops, but antiaircraft fire hit pilots, crew and the attacking troops. Suppressive fire from the Black Hawks was ineffective because of their violent maneuvers. Although some Rangers walked away from the crashed and damaged Black Hawks, others were badly hurt and were not immediately evacuated. Part of the evacuation problem seems to have been that Army pilots could not land aboard Navy ships because they were not qualified to do so, although this was eventually waived.

Intelligence failed at the prison and also when the Rangers were not informed until 1030 on the morning of 25 October that there were still students at the second campus at Grand Anse. Students reported guards in the area, but the Rangers thought they could bring the students out. A heliborne operation with Marine airlift from the *Guam* was planned. Marine Helicopter Squadron 261 was to provide the helicopters, with supporting fire from USAF C-130 gunships, ships off the coast, and the Marines' two remaining Cobra attack helicopters. American suppressive fire would continue until twenty seconds before the Rangers were committed.

The Rangers would fly to the objective in three waves, each composed of three CH-46s. Each wave of three would carry a company of Rangers, about fifty men. A Company would go in first, followed by B Company, which was to cordon off the campus to prevent outside intervention. C Company would then arrive, its mission to locate the students and pack them into the four CH-53s waiting offshore.

During lift-off the order of aircraft somehow became confused. Instead of the lead flight having three CH-46s carrying A Company, the first wave had one from A Company and two from B Company. Consequently, the second wave had two from A and one from B. The first three aircraft missed the designated beach in front of the campus. There was sporadic small arms fire, but the only serious damage came from overhanging trees. One helicopter shut down and was abandoned in the surf, but the Rangers scrambled out as water poured in. Later, a second machine was damaged by a tree.

The orbiting Sea Stallions were now brought in to remove the students. The CH-46s returned and extracted the Rangers, completing the entire operation in twenty-six minutes. After leaving the beach, they realized that eleven men sent up the beach as a flank guard had not returned. By radio these men were told to move toward positions held by the 82nd Airborne. The Rangers were not sure they could safely enter those lines, so they decided to use one of the inflatable boats from the disabled helicopter. However, the rafts had been damaged during the air assault. The Rangers soon had to swim alongside their damaged boat. Having battled surf and tides for some time, they were spotted, picked up at 2300, and brought to the USS *Caron* lying off the coast.

One of the Rangers' initial D-day objectives, Calivigny Barracks, had not been secured. Lying about five kilometers from the airfield, the barracks reportedly housed and trained troops. On 27 October, under the command of a Brigade headquarters from the 82nd Airborne Division, a full-scale attack was carried out by Company B, 2/75, reinforced by Company C, 1/75.

Four waves of four Black Hawks, each carrying a company to assault the camp, were to fly out to sea before heading to the beach, flying low over the water at about 100 knots. Support was furnished by Spectre gunships and Navy A-7s. At

Salines the Army had seventeen 105mm howitzers, and at sea the USS *Caron* would supply fire support. A Company, 2/75, was to land at the southern end of the compound, on the left, and on the right, C Company, 2/75, was to set down. B Company, 2/75, was to land in the southeast, assault suspected antiaircraft guns, and rejoin the other companies in the north. In reserve was C Company, 1/75, which would also hold the southern end of the perimeter.

The Black Hawks came in over the waves, climbing sharply to the top of the cliffs. Quickly, the pilots slowed down in order to find the exact landing zone inside the perimeter. Each Black Hawk came in rapidly, one behind the other. The first helicopter put down safely, near the southern boundary of the camp, and was followed by the second. Rangers began to dismount. The third Black Hawk suffered some damage, and spun forward, smashing into the second machine. In the fourth Black Hawk, the crew saw what was happening and veered hard right; the aircraft landed in a ditch, damaging its tail rotor. Apparently not realizing that the helicopter's rotor was damaged, the pilot attempted to move the Black Hawk, which rose sharply, seemed to spin forward, and crashed. In twenty seconds three machines were down. Debris and rotor blades flew through the air, badly wounding four Rangers and killing three who, sadly, were the only deaths in the 2/75.

A Company regrouped as C Company landed on large concrete pads on the edge of the compound. B Company also landed safely, and moved on its objective. C Company, 1/75, also landed without incident. Contrary to expectations, the barracks were deserted. The Rangers found nothing. That night they slept in the rubble caused by the intense bombardment. This was their last action before returning to the United States.

Panama Invasion

The Army learned much from the confusion in Grenada. Special Operations Command (SOCOM) was established in 1984 to coordinate special operations. Air assault missions similar to the invasion were practiced and planned for several years before it took place. On 17 December 1989, Gen. Karl Steiner alerted specific units to prepare for an operation. Cargo planes began to arrive at Pope Air Force Base, North Carolina. On 18 December the Rangers moved to Green Ramp at Pope, where they were isolated to prevent information leaks. Other airborne units also arrived at Green Ramp. On 19 December, General Steiner flew to Panama.

The Rangers were to secure Torillos International Airport, Rio Hata Military Airfield, and then Noriega's beach house. Rangers who dropped into the International Airport later moved into Panama City, where they took the military headquarters of the Panamanian Defense Forces.

The jump into Rio Hata airfield was made under fire at an altitude of 500ft. Heavy antiaircraft fire was encountered and one Ranger was hit in the back of the head while still in the airplane. He survived, but four Rangers were killed in this operation. The Rangers secured the perimeter of the field before the Panamanians began to test the defenses. At Rio Hata the Rangers were supported by AC-130 Spectre gunships, whose target acquisition cameras found targets in the dark. Two hours after the drop at Rio Hata, the airfield was secure enough for transport aircraft to begin landing with supplies and additional equipment for the Rangers.

Once the airfields were secure, the Rangers moved against the Panamanian special forces, the Mountain Troops. Rangers moved from house to house in the compound, and at the village where the families of the soldiers lived. Many of the Mountain Troops were caught while trying to shave off their distinctive beards. On the fifth day of the operation the Rangers were sent to secure Calle Diez, an area some twenty to twenty-five miles from Panama City, held by the "Dignity Battalions."

Rangers took many pictures of Panamanian and foreign property, aircraft, shops, and houses to show that property was still intact and protected by the US Army. This prevented false claims and probably saved the United States many hundreds of thousands of dollars. Rangers also guarded buildings—such as the Vatican Embassy where President Noriega took refuge—to see that no damage was done. Twenty days after the start of the operation the Rangers left Panama.

Desert Storm

Very little is known about Ranger participation in Desert Storm, 1991. Delta Company of the 4th Ranger Training Battalion sent a squad to train members of the 24th Infantry Division (mechanized) to carry out long-range surveillance (LRS) operations in the desert. One incident proved the effectiveness of the training. Two teams in surveillance holes about 125 miles behind enemy lines the second day of the ground war spotted a squad of Iraqi soldiers with an armored reconnaissance vehicle approaching. For forty-five minutes the Iraqis surveyed the area, coming as close as ten feet to the camouflaged holes. The LRS teams were not detected and the Iraqis moved on.

Company B and one platoon of Company A, 1/75, took part in special operations in the desert. We can only surmise that they carried out missions against radar and communications installations, and hunted Scuds, especially after the attacks on Israel. The Rangers may also have secured airfields in Iraq for use by other special forces. All these missions are consistent with Ranger training. The rest of the Ranger Regiment was held in reserve for contingency operations.

In December 1991, Company C, 1/75, and the Regimental Headquarters Company deployed to Kuwait for a routine training exercise. The Rangers jumped into Kuwait during daylight hours, which is not typical, so television news cameras could record their arrival. The daylight jump also reminded Saddam Hussein that the United States was capable of quickly responding to any further threats to the security of the region.

Chapter 2

Ranger Training Brigade

The Ranger Department of the Infantry School at Fort Benning, Georgia, was established in 1951 to provide individual Ranger training to officers and noncommissioned officers (NCOs). Graduates earned the right to wear, on their left shoulder, a curved, yellow on black strip, or tab, that said "Ranger." Students were trained at Fort Benning in patrolling, ambushes, raids, airborne operations, and leadership skills. Physical training was also emphasized. Mountain training was moved from Colorado to Dahlonega, Georgia, and a jungle phase conducted at Eglin Air Force Base, Florida, was added. The first class to earn the Ranger tab graduated in March 1952.

The Ranger Department was reorganized in 1958 into three companies: 1st Ranger Company, Florida Ranger Division; 2nd Ranger Company, Mountain Ranger Division; and 3rd Ranger Company, Benning Ranger Division. Desert training was instituted in 1983, first at Fort Bliss, Texas, and then in 1985 at Dugway Proving Grounds, Utah. On 13 September 1991 the desert phase was moved back to Fort Bliss. The change was made because the Utah desert, which is a high plateau desert, becomes too cold in the winter to provide an environment similar to that of the Middle East.

On 5 August 1987, the Ranger Department was separated from the Infantry School and reestablished as the Ranger Training Brigade. The Ranger companies now became the 4th Ranger Training Battalion, Fort Benning; 5th Ranger Training Battalion, Dahlonega; 6th Ranger Training Battalion, Eglin; and the 7th Ranger Training Battalion, Fort Bliss. The training schedule was fifty-eight days before the desert phase and sixty-five days after. Starting with the class of 1-92, 14 October 1991, the training schedule was increased to sixty-eight days. The original training rotation was Fort Benning, Dahlonega, Eglin, and Dugway. With the 1-92 class, the sequence became Fort Benning, Fort Bliss, Dahlonega, and Eglin, with about sixteen days at each phase. The rest of the time is devoted to travel and processing.

With the establishment of the Ranger Training Department in 1952, the emphasis of Ranger training shifted from the company level to the individual. The idea became to transmit Ranger training to the rest of the Army by training officers and NCOs who would return to their units and teach what they had been taught. The original goal was to have one Ranger NCO per platoon and one Ranger officer per company by graduating 3,000 Rangers a year. However, with the dropout rate remaining steady at approximately sixty-five percent, the goal was not usually met. In 1984 the Army investigated the idea of making Ranger training mandatory for officers. This was rejected because a mandatory program would reduce the enthusiasm and morale of the students and dilute the value of the Ranger tab. The honor associated with the tab, and its utility in career advancement, would keep high the number of volunteers.

The goal of Ranger training, according to the commander's brief, is "to produce a hardened, competent, small-unit leader who is confident he can lead his unit into combat and overcome all obstacles to accomplish his mission" by requiring them to "perform effectively as small-unit leaders in tactically realistic environments." Upon graduation, the student knows that, when necessary, he can reach down into himself to do whatever is required to get the job done and get his men out alive. When you've earned your Ranger tab, as one sergeant put it, "you know you'll be able to do anything, even if it's something you've never done before and know absolutely nothing about. That doesn't matter. You're a Ranger, you can do anything!"

To produce a realistic environment, the stress of combat is simulated by hunger, lack of sleep, constant pressure, and a grueling physical setting. The long training day, usually from 0500 hours to 0200 hours, makes judgment difficult, similar to when in battle. The short rations—one or two MREs (meals ready to eat) a day after the Fort Benning phase—add further problems. The average weight loss per student is thirty pounds. Live fire exercises were stopped in early 1991 because the students come from all of the armed forces and do not have enough training as a unit to be sure of each others' responses when shooting live ammunition. The students are expected to go from squad to platoon to company level operations as they get physically weaker and mentally confused. By the end of the course, the student is in the worst physical shape of his life.

While the Ranger school trains individuals, teamwork is essential to pass. The concept of working with your Ranger buddy is constantly emphasized. All tasks are done by two-man teams. If your buddy has trouble, you don't continue until he is ready. Cooperation within the platoon is also stressed. Passing the course does not depend on the failure of others. Those platoons with the most cooperation have the highest rates of graduation. Within the course all students are equal regardless of rank and all have the same chance of success or failure.

All male officers and noncommissioned officers (sergeant and above) from American and allied services are eligible to apply for Ranger training. Anyone below these ranks must obtain a waiver from the first colonel (O6 grade) in his chain of command. All applicants must be in good

Students jump into the Ranger Training Camp at Dugway Proving Grounds, Utah, for the desert phase of training. The camp was moved to Utah in 1985, but in 1991 it was returned to Fort Bliss to take advantage of the fort's better support facilities. US Army

health and top physical condition. Certain conditions such as any hypothermia injury are grounds for disqualification. Airborne qualifications are desirable but not required. Students come from all branches of the armed services of the United States and allied countries. Approximately sixty percent come from the US Army, twenty percent from other US services, and twenty percent from foreign countries.

4th Ranger Training Battalion, Fort Benning, Georgia

Training is conducted at Fort Benning in two phases. The first five days of training, mainly processing and testing, occur at Camp Rogers, named for Robert Rogers of Rogers' Rangers fame. This is a garrison in which the students live in barracks and eat in the mess hall. The Ranger Training Brigade and the 4th Ranger Training Battalion are headquartered here.

For the remainder of the Fort Benning phase, ten days, training is conducted at Camp Darby, named for William O. Darby, the founder of the modern Rangers. The camp, with few permanent structures, is located deep in the wooded hills of Fort Benning. Each company has its own rudimentary facilities in quanset hut structures. The students live and eat in the open.

Under the eyes of a Ranger instructor (RI), new students demonstrate their ability to maintain an M16 rifle. The Ranger Stakes were instituted in 1991 to test the students' familiarity with light infantry weapons and communications. Seven of the eleven tasks must be successfully completed to pass. The students get two tries at each task. The RIs retrain and retest those who fail the first time. A second failure counts.

Besides the "prisoner of war" camp, there are five permanent sites used for field training exercises. The largest is Cinder Block Village, which, as its name implies, contains two bare, partitioned buildings and a wooden tower, completely surrounded by a chain-link fence. The other sites, some of which contain small bunkers, simulate objectives such as missile installations and communications facilities. The Darby Queen obstacle course is the only other permanent installation.

The new student reports to the Ranger Training Brigade with his medical and military records, but without his rank or service insignia. After the in-processing paperwork is completed, each student takes the Army Physical Fitness Test—fifty-two push-ups, sixty-two sit-ups, and a two-mile run in running shoes in less than fourteen minutes and fifty-five seconds. He must also do six chin-ups. The majority of entering students pass without problems.

The next test facing the student is the combat water survival test which consists of three events. The first, the fifteen-meter swim, must be completed wearing fatigues, boots, and web equipment such as canteens and ammunition pouches, and carrying a rifle, without loss of rifle or equipment —and without showing undue fear or panic. Next, the student must submerge and remain underwa-

Retesting a student on his ability to load an M60 machine gun. If the student fails again, this stake will be a no-go. If the student fails five stakes, he is dropped from the course. He may recycle in the next class if he wishes.

Students prepare M18A1 Claymore mines for detonation. They will run the wires back to positions about twenty-five yards in the rear and then detonate the mines. Knowledge of mines is important for many Ranger-type missions.

ter while discarding rifle and equipment and swim to poolside—again without undue fear or panic. Finally, the student, while blindfolded, must walk off the end of a three-meter diving board, remove the blindfold, and swim to poolside without loss of equipment or rifle. While some fear or panic is normal, an undue amount results in an automatic drop. Undue or unusual fear or panic is defined as more than the average, intelligent man feels. The students are then assigned to the three companies of the 4th Ranger Training Battalion. The rest of the first day is taken up with equipment issue and more paperwork.

The students are now assigned buddies. A pair of Ranger buddies works together throughout the training course. If one falls behind, the other is expected to help him. No Ranger does anything alone. He and his buddy work as a team. This concept goes back to the "Me and My Pal" training of Darby's Rangers during World War II. Ideally, Ranger buddies stay together until graduation, but many change buddies at least once because of

Ranger students returning from a predawn run. During the Ranger Assessment Phase (RAP) at Fort Benning, students must complete the five-mile run to continue the course. The runs, as well as all other activities, are conducted by companies. Each student, upon arrival, is assigned to A, B, or C Company of the 4th Ranger Training Battalion. During later phases of training, runs are not graded separately but are part of overall training.

medical drops and failures. Ranger buddies often remain friends for life, regardless of rank.

The first five days of the Fort Benning phase of the Ranger Training Course are known as the Ranger Assessment Phase (RAP). Previous to the class of 1-92, students would begin training conditions almost immediately, including twenty-hour days and grueling physical training (PT). While PT is still stressed, the new RAP schedule calls for a more relaxed environment while testing the students in a five-mile run in forty minutes, day and night land navigation, and a new series of tests known as the Ranger Stakes.

The Ranger Stakes was added because many of the students from other services and countries may not be familiar with US Army equipment and weapons. The Ranger instructors (RIs) found that it was too time-consuming and too distracting to teach the proper use of weapons and equipment at the same time as carrying on Ranger training. The Ranger Stakes provides a quick test of students' abilities and an opportunity to remedy any deficiencies on the spot. Those who fail are trained immediately and retested. Most students pass the retest.

The Ranger Stakes consists of eleven tasks, grouped into five parts, that test students on their ability to handle communications and light infantry weapons.

The first three Stakes tasks test ability with the M60 machine gun. A student must show he can maintain an M60 by taking it apart and putting it back together in a reasonable time. The time is determined by the RI in charge. A student from an Army unit is expected to be quicker at this task than someone from another service that does not regularly use the M60. The second task is to load an M60. The third task is to prepare a range card for an M60 machine gun. To prevent accidents to one's own troops and to cover every field of fire, M60s and similar weapons are usually sighted to fire within an arc of several degrees. A properly prepared range card allows the gun to be manned by more than one person if necessary. The card shows the angle the gun is set at from the position of the operator.

Task number four is to employ an M181A1 Claymore mine. The mine is detonated electrically using a wire. Students must set the mine and then run the wire back about twenty-five yards, connect it to the electric detonator, and set it off. Of course the whole process is a simulation.

Tasks five and six involve communications. Students must send a radio message and encode and decode a message using the standard KTC 600 operations code. Foreign students who are not proficient in English sometimes have difficulty with these tasks.

Students negotiate the infamous worm pit before dawn on the confidence course. They crawl on their backs and on their bellies under knee-high barbed wire through a pit of mud. The RIs keep the mud soft with generous applications from a garden hose.

The next three Stakes involve the basic weapon of the Army and of the Rangers—the M16 rifle. Tasks seven and eight are to demonstrate the ability to maintain and correct malfunctions of an M16. Number nine is to perform a functions check on an M16. A Ranger is expected to maintain his M16 in good condition at all times. During training exercises, students do not rest before cleaning and checking their rifles.

The last two Stakes involve grenades. Number ten is to employ hand grenades and number eleven, the ability to maintain an M203 grenade launcher.

The Ranger Stakes are held the morning and afternoon of the second day of training. Students must pass seven of the eleven tasks to continue. Those who fail are immediately given training by an RI and retested. A second failure of a task is final. Over ninety percent pass the Stakes on the first or second try. Those few who fail more than four Stakes may recycle with the next class and try again.

The morning of the third day, after the pre-dawn run, which is held every day at a pace of eight minutes per mile, the students tackle the confidence course which builds agility and endurance. The students first climb a four-meter-high log fence without the aid of ropes. Then they enter the worm pit, a shallow, muddy 25m length area covered by knee-high barbed wire. The students must crawl on their backs and bellies *under* the wire while the RIs keep the mud fresh with water from garden hoses.

Next, the students must cross another mud pit by going hand-over-hand on the rafters in the roof of the five-meter-long pit. Falling, even at the end, means you have to do it over again. The rafters, 10ft above the pit, become so slippery with mud that the last few students across are allowed to use their legs as well as their arms.

The last obstacle is loosely rigged rope netting. The students climb the netting and then slide down a rope on the other side. The companies that finish first usually do push-ups or run in place until the others are finished. Even in the coldest weather, the students are only too glad to wash off under the outdoor faucets and change into dry uniforms.

The students are tested on their map-and-compass navigation skills the third and fourth days. They are marched or trucked to an area away from Camp Rogers and then given a few hours to reach a coordinate on their maps. Only one compass per student is allowed. Any student found with more than one compass is immediately dropped from the course. The compass must be standard issue. Students may not use any other type. There is one daylight land navigation test and one night test. Those who fail are retested. Those

After the worm pit, a student attempts to cross a muddy pool by swinging from rafter to rafter. If he falls into the mud, he has to start again. The last company of students coming through is allowed to use their feet to stay aloft because the rafters usually become too slippery to grasp.

Students on the netting, which is the last part of the confidence course. While it is not one of the critical tasks that must be passed, the confidence course is not taken lightly. If he fails, a student is sent to take it over and over until he passes.

who fail the retest are dropped but may recycle in the next class.

Those students who fail any phase of Ranger training and decide to recycle may remain at the headquarters where they failed and join the Gulag. While waiting to join the next class, the members of the Gulag receive remedial training. They also perform routine tasks such as ground and building maintenance and improvements. The Gulag also aids the opposing forces (opfor) when necessary during field training exercises. Camp Rogers has the largest Gulag because it has the greatest number of students in a class and thus the largest number of medical and training drops.

The Ranger Assessment Phase ends with the water confidence test. The students climb a crude ladder, walk across a log thirty feet above the ground, and then drop from a rope 35ft into Victory Pond. Immediately afterward, the students climb up a 60ft tower and slide down a 200ft inclined rope back into the water. The water confidence test is conducted summer and winter unless the water temperature is less than 39deg Fahrenheit or the air temperature and wind chill are lower than 38deg Fahrenheit.

The RIs believe that the way a student walks across the log indicates the way he will behave in a combat situation. Those who walk firmly and without hesitation will do well. Those who hesitate or show fear may not. Occasionally, a student will try to show off for the RIs. One student who jumped over the two steps in the middle of the log was told to repeat the jump at least twice more for the benefit of those who didn't see it. The RI in charge then made the student hang from the rope longer than the others before being allowed to drop. Showoffs may be fun to watch, but they can be dangerous on a mission.

During the first five days of Ranger school, the students practice unarmed hand-to-hand combat in the evenings. Compared to more formal and stylized systems, Ranger methods may seem crude, but they are efficient. The students learn to use their fists, elbows, knees, feet—any part of the body that can be effective against an opponent. Working in pairs, the students practice for three or four hours at a time. During rest breaks, the RIs show how it's done and talk about what the students can expect in training. Some RIs like to play inspirational music during breaks; the scores from the movies *Apocalypse Now* and *Patton* are popular choices.

The Camp Darby phase of Ranger school begins with a parachute jump from helicopters into a clearing near the camp's permanent structures. Those students who are not airborne qualified are trucked to the clearing. This jump was instituted with the 1992 curriculum to familiarize the class with the type of airborne operations usually conducted by Rangers.

For the first three days the students receive classroom instruction in the fundamentals of patrolling, advanced land navigation, troop leading procedures, and leadership responsibilities. RIs also conduct battle drills. Physical training continues daily. Runs at an eight-minute-per-mile pace are included, but are not graded separately from the other training.

On the fourth day, the students tackle the Darby Queen obstacle course: twenty obstacles strewn up and down a densely wooded hillside. They crawl, run, jump, climb, and slide through the obstacles with their Ranger buddies, helping each other where necessary. If your buddy doesn't make it over an obstacle, you don't continue until he does. In between the obstacles, the RIs usually have the students do push-ups, the most common activity in any phase of Ranger training.

The afternoon is devoted to survival training. The class learns how to catch and cook rabbits and

A company of Ranger students engaged in the most common activity in all phases of Ranger school. Frequent push-ups are part of the physical conditioning program.

other fauna when no other provisions are available. The RIs deliberately did not allow the class to eat anything earlier that day so the students will not hesitate to eat their catches.

The remaining time at Camp Darby is spent on reconnaissance field training exercises using the crawl/walk/run method. The RIs first demonstrate the techniques and then guide the students through them. This is the crawl stage. During the walk stage students practice under the observation of the instructors. The run stage is a field training exercise which is graded. Crawl/walk/run training is an effective way to develop skills quickly.

A Ranger student tries to do push-ups in the "koala" position. Push-ups, especially in awkward positions, are common as a disciplinary measure.

The opfor for the field training exercises are played by the Merrills, a platoon of the 4th Ranger Training Battalion Headquarters Company. The Merrills use captured Eastern Bloc or non-standard weapons and equipment to simulate a realistic enemy force. They occupy the various sites used during the exercises, patrolling and setting guards to detect intruders. Any students caught during missions are interned in the prisoner of war camp, which is also as realistic as feasible. The Merrills are the largest opfor at any of the training battalions because the 4th has the largest number of students at any time.

The students are given operations orders by squads and conduct day and night reconnaissance missions the last four days. If they are spotted, they run the risk of being "killed" or captured. During the field training exercises students receive only one MRE per day, two in the winter cycle, and a bread supplement. On the sixteenth day of Ranger school, the class flies out to Fort Bliss, Texas, for two weeks of desert training.

7th Ranger Training Battalion, Fort Bliss, Texas

The second phase of Ranger school, the desert phase, begins with in-flight rigging for a parachute jump upon arrival. Those students who are not jump-qualified join the rest of the class when the transports land. The garrison part of desert training, which lasts five days, begins the next day. During this phase, students receive three meals a day and get about five hours of sleep a night. The Ranger camp, located on the McGregor Range at Fort Bliss, will be named Camp Schocklee for the command sergeant major of the 7th Training Battalion killed in a parachute accident at Dugway, Utah.

The students learn desert-survival techniques such as water procurement and preservation. The RIs conduct classes reviewing leadership responsibilities and standing operating procedures for platoons. Each company of students spends one day practicing reconnaissance techniques and ambushes after classroom reviews.

Another day is spent practicing some battle drills important for Ranger operations. The drills are coordinated movement patterns such as flanking actions or turns that are usually executed as a reaction to enemy action. They are standard throughout the US Army. These include reacting to contact with the enemy, reacting to indirect (unobserved) fire, and reacting to ambush. The RIs also conduct platoon attack drills.

7th Ranger Training Battalion support personnel act as the opfor for these and all other exercises. During the garrison phase the members of the opfor who are killed in action are predetermined. This ensures that there will be bodies to search for booby traps and secure captured weapons and equipment. During the field exercises, casualties among the opfor and the students depend on the circumstances.

During the first week of desert training, students learn how to penetrate barbed wire without injury with wire cutters, or with makeshift ladders when necessary. They learn how to clear a trench line, working in two-man teams, each covering the other. They are also taught how to assault a fortified bunker.

The RIs teach how to ambush men and vehicles. The students alternate classroom lectures with walk-through exercises. The instructors stress the importance of mastering a technique until it becomes second nature. Only then should a leader try out other ways of ambushing. This holds true for any activity that is not a battle drill, which can only be executed one way.

All training is conducted with METT-T factors emphasized. M(ission) E(nemy) T(errain) T(roops)-T(ime available) must be taken into account whenever an operation is conducted. Even the most foolproof plan will not work if these factors are neglected. Throughout the remainder of training phases, the students will be constantly urged to remember METT-T when planning their field exercises.

On the afternoon of the sixth day of desert training, the field training exercises begin. The students will carry out reconnaissance, conduct raids, and mount ambushes. The class will participate in an airborne operation, parachuting to the target. There will also be an air assault from helicopters. The culmination of desert training is an airborne assault with full class participation. Students who are not airborne qualified are trucked to the jump site to take part. Meals are now reduced to one MRE a day.

Two RIs demonstrate hand-to-hand combat. The man on the ground appears to be defeated, but in a moment he will throw his adversary by pulling on the upper arm and kicking upward.

Except for the night before a parachute jump when five hours sleep is mandated, most students get only one or two hours of sleep during field training exercises. Those who do their assigned tasks, including maintaining their weapons, more efficiently can grab a little more rest. The company, platoon, and squad leaders for each exercise who must plan the mission get the least sleep. By the fourteenth day of desert training, after six days in the field, the men are operating on instinct and training.

When the desert phase ends, on the thirty-third day of Ranger school, the class flies back to Fort Benning for the bus ride to Camp Merrill, Dahlonega, Georgia. Only about sixty percent of the original class will go on to mountain training. The remaining forty percent will have dropped out for medical reasons such as injury or illness. Some will have failed critical tasks or leadership evaluations. Those who wish may join the next class after recovery or retraining. This option is available at all phases of training.

5th Ranger Training Battalion, Dahlonega, Georgia

The mountain training phase is divided into lower and upper mountaineering, mountain techniques, and tactical operations. The first three days are spent in and around Camp Frank D. Merrill, named for the leader of the Marauders. Again, during the garrison part of training, students receive two hot meals and one MRE a day, and around five or six hours sleep a night.

The students learn various knots needed to secure ropes and climbing equipment. The knots are also important for securing explosives and rigging fuses. Rope handling and belaying (stopping movement on a climb) are taught on level ground.

A 20ft wall built of wooden slats is used to teach rappelling, including the Australian method where the climber appears to be walking straight down the slope face forward. Students learn how to secure their lines to a fixed point above the wall or to insert metal rings where no other anchor is available.

Next, students practice rappelling down a sixty-foot cliff, with and without rucksacks. They also learn how to carry an injured comrade while rappelling. To successfully pass this part of training students must perform three daytime rappels, including one with full rucksack, and one using only two bounces against the cliff. A nighttime rappel with full rucksack is also required. During the winter months rain and cold turn the cliff face

The RI in charge of hand-to-hand combat training shows off his skills with fighting sticks before the class starts. The use of such sticks is not taught to the students.

An RI throws his "enemy" into Victory Pond during a Rangers-in-action performance. Four or five times a year, on the morning of a Ranger school graduation, the instructors and opposing forces (opfor) at the 4th Ranger Training Battalion demonstrate the skills of Rangers to the incoming class and the public. The performance includes use of weapons and explosives, rappelling skills, and insertion and extraction by helicopter into a heavily wooded area.

into a sheet of ice. When this happens, a fixed rope descent is substituted for the night rappel. But the three daytime ones are still performed.

The fifth and sixth days of mountain training are spent on the top of Mount Yonah, the highest peak in Georgia. There, students learn how to climb, as well as descend. They learn how to use safety lines and transport equipment and all the skills necessary for mountain operations. The next two days are spent back at Camp Merrill.

During the time in garrison, physical training is not neglected. Every day begins with a run. Distances vary, but the pace is never less than eight minutes per mile—the Army standard. Often, the pace is quicker. Beside the ubiquitous push-ups, other calisthenics are part of the daily routine. One Ranger remembers during training that it "seemed we spent half our time in the flutter kick position and the other half doing push-ups."

The field training exercises in the mountains, which start on the eighth day, are tactical operations on the platoon and company levels. The students plan and execute reconnaissance, ambushes, raids, airborne operations, and air assaults as in other phases, but the mountains make these exercises more difficult. Movement along inclines and ridgelines is more difficult; rope bridges are sometimes needed. Helicopters must land in small mountain clearings completely surrounded by trees.

Airborne operations are more challenging. The drop zones for parachute jumps are the smallest throughout the Ranger Training Brigade. One, Garrett's Farm, is only 150 meters by 100 meters—with a stream and a Y-shaped band of trees running through the middle. Not surprisingly, the RIs and support personnel carry special tools to extract men and parachutes from trees.

All these factors result in more medical drops due to injuries than in any other phase. Sprains, pulled or torn muscles, and dislocations are common. Every part of the body that can be broken will be. Even those who do not sustain more serious injuries collect scrapes and bruises. As in the other phases, students are allowed to miss a day of training to rest or recover from a minor injury. Anything requiring more time results in a drop, with the opportunity to recycle.

The field exercises follow a pattern throughout all phases of training. The company leader and the platoon leaders receive orders for a mission and then devise a plan to carry it out successfully. The squad leaders are expected to add their input to the plan. If weather or other natural factors prevent the completion of the mission or cause it to fail, the mission will still receive a "go" (pass) if the students have tried their best to continue. Leadership rotates among the students so that each may be evaluated at least once in every phase of training. A student in danger of failing is usually given more time as leader in the later phases so that he may improve his performance.

The members of the opfor at Camp Merrill live in the field for the eight days of the field exercises.

Two RIs rehearse before a hand-to-hand class. The RI on the right is parrying the attack with his left hand while counterpunching with his right.

A student crawls under a barbed-wire obstacle on the Darby Queen. Ranger students seem to spend much of their time crawling through dirt and mud.

Another part of Ranger physical training—endless flutter kicks.

The trailer that impersonates a communications base during raids serves as the men's field quarters. Its interior sleeps eight on bunks that double as storage shelves. Battery-powered lights, food, water bottles, a small propane stove, and a few radios make life in the field as comfortable as possible. The men hope to hook up to an electrical source so they can add a television.

The opfor carefully plan their ambushes against the students for maximum effect. The students are attacked by a group in the treeline on a mountain landing zone as they exit the helicopters. To ambush a student company returning to camp for the mandatory sleep the night before a parachute jump, three or four men of the opfor conceal themselves among the bushes just past a bend in the road. They wait silently, often on wet and muddy ground on the side of the mountain, not moving for fear of revealing their position. After the advance squads of students pass, the opfor attack. The foggy evening adds to the confusion as the students scatter. A few squad leaders who manage to keep their men together and return fire receive positive spot reports.

On the forty-ninth day of the Ranger Training Course, the class travels by bus to Eglin Air Force Base, Florida, for jungle training. Less than half of the students have made it so far. At this point, students are totally immersed in the training. They are tired, hungry, and generally grungy. All thoughts of the soft, outside world have faded. Fast food burgers, the PX, movies, and the NCO club have been replaced by an M16, the rappelling ropes, and MREs. And the most grueling part of the training still lies ahead.

6th Ranger Training Battalion, Eglin Air Force Base, Florida

Camp James E. Rudder, on Eglin Air Force Base, is named for the commander of the 2nd Ranger Battalion who led the assault on Pointe du Hoe. Here, Ranger students learn to cope with a

An RI demonstrates the use of elbows and feet to fend off an opponent.

During RAP at Fort Benning, students are taught the fundamentals of unarmed hand-to-hand combat. The students assume the basic stance for attack or defense. Pantlegs are rolled outside the boots to prevent injury.

jungle and swamp environment. The high humidity of the north Florida coast adds to the rigors of training. To the physically and mentally tired students who arrive the night before the fiftieth day of training, the camp seems damp: hot and damp in summer and cold and damp in winter.

Students have a busy first day. In outdoor classrooms, they review patrol base operations and review the duties and responsibilities of platoon leaders and platoon sergeants. They go over the mechanics of zone reconnaissance. The cadre of the 6th Ranger Training Battalion demonstrate ambush and raid techniques.

For the first time in their training, the students are introduced to movement-to-contact tactics. The RIs and support personnel demonstrate how to move through terrain in expectation of encountering enemy forces and how to continue movement after engagement. This is taught only after the students have mastered patrolling and reconnaissance in the earlier portions of training.

The first day ends with another class. This one deals with reptiles—snakes and alligators—how to identify and avoid them. Students also learn first aid to treat snakebites. The 6th Battalion keeps a snake house and alligator pond at headquarters to facilitate training.

Days two and three are spent in the field, practicing raids, ambushes, and movement to contact. The companies, reduced by attrition to platoon size, spend the two nights in patrol bases. While these are not considered field exercises, the conditions are similar. Meals are MREs and sleep lasts a maximum of four hours. The days do not start with physical training.

The fourth day of training is devoted to stream crossings and small-boat operations. Until class 1-92, learning to use ropes to cross streams with men and equipment was conducted at Camp Rudder. Now, with the increase in field training exercises in Florida, rope crossings are taught at Fort Benning and Dahlonega. The cool streams are a welcome relief from the heat in summer, but are cold in winter.

The students practice on land first. Then, accompanied by RIs, they paddle squad-sized Zodiac boats to patrol bases in the swamp, where they will spend the night. During the field training

The defending student (on the left) ducks under the attacker's blow. The RI is commenting on their performance. Although Ranger techniques may seem crude, they are effective.

A student walks the log during the water confidence test. The log is thirty feet above ground over Victory Pond. The RIs say the way a man walks the log is the way he will behave in combat. Those who hesitate may also hesitate when on a mission.

After the log, the students hang from a rope suspended thirty-five feet above the pond. They cannot drop into the water until the RI in charge says so. Sometimes, the RIs will make a particularly confident student untie his boots or place both hands in his pockets before giving permission. If a student drops prematurely, he is usually made to climb out and crawl through the mud to the next part of the water confidence test.

exercises, which start now, the boats will be used on rivers and in the open waters of the Gulf of Mexico.

During the field training exercises, the class conducts operations similar to the other phases: reconnaissance, raids, ambushes, airborne operations, and air assaults. Movement to contact and small-boat operations are now added. The three platoon-sized companies conduct separate and joint exercises. For the next nine days the students spend all their time in the swamps. Meals are limited to one MRE daily. Sleep is almost nonexistent. The only break is the night before a parachute jump, when they are allowed five hours sleep in the barracks.

The Florida phase is the most challenging. Ranger students, already exhausted and dazed, must expend whatever strength remains simply to move through the swamps and jungles. Thought becomes almost impossible, planning difficult. Those who will have hallucinations will usually have them in Florida. Students "see" all kinds of food. Bushes and trees become people. Students

A student slides down a 200ft rope into Victory Pond. At the RI's signal, the student will drop from the rope into the water. The red float on his back will enable a rescue team to haul him out if he sticks in the mud on the pond's bottom.

may walk in their sleep or even try to attack an imagined enemy. Students must rely on mental toughness to see themselves through. Those who lack it quit, even at the very end. Some students reach Santa Rosa Island at the end of the field training exercises and quit the course. They don't care that the only task left is graduation. They have had enough. Those who make it know that they have the strength to face anything.

The field training exercises and the Ranger course end with a predawn assault on Santa Rosa Island. Students start their preparations around 1600 hours. The zodiac boats are checked and loaded. Last-minute plans are reviewed. The three companies coordinate their attack. The boats set off at dark to cross the open stretch of water between the Florida Panhandle and the island. Around 0400 hours the boats reach the island. Suddenly, a barrage of flares, simulating supporting fire, lights up the beach as the Ranger students fight their way ashore. After the final after-action report, the only task left is to return to Camp

A student exits a Black Hawk helicopter. Those students who are airborne-qualified jump into Camp Darby to begin the next part of their training. This jump is the first one into Darby under the new curriculum. Previous classes did not begin the Darby phase with a jump. But as most Ranger activities usually involve a helicopter jump, the 4th Training Brigade added one at this point. After the jump, a student walks to his assigned assembly point.

A student jumps over a log while his buddy waits his turn. The Darby Queen obstacle course, located on a wooded hillside in Camp Darby, is one of the critical tasks required for graduation from Ranger school. The Darby Queen requires motor skills similar to those used in combat situations—running, jumping, climbing, and crawling. The men of the 75th Ranger Regiment negotiate the Darby Queen as part of their physical exercises.

The students negotiate the Darby Queen in pairs: if your buddy gets stuck at an obstacle, you don't continue until he does. Some obstacles such as the four-level platform cannot be negotiated without cooperation. The Ranger buddy system originated during World War II, when Darby's men trained in pairs.

Rudder and prepare for the trip back to Camp Rogers where it all started.

The next day, the sixty-eighth, the students return to Fort Benning, hungry and exhausted, to feast on steak and shrimp and get a rare full night's sleep. Those who have made it to this point will graduate in the morning. Graduation day is its own reward. Field music, parading colors, and admiring families all add to the fierce pride and esprit de corps the Army's newest Rangers feel as the long weeks of rigorous training culminate in the awarding of the coveted black and yellow Ranger tab.

A C-141 drops airborne-qualified students into the new desert training camp at McGregor Range, Fort Bliss, Texas, for the second phase of Ranger school.

Completing the Ranger Training Course

Less than thirty percent of those who begin complete the Ranger Training Course with the class they started. Half never earn the tab. There are many ways to fail. A student must receive one positive leadership evaluation in each phase. He must pass a minimum of one patrol each in the desert, mountains, and jungle, and a total of fifty percent of all combat operations (exercises) at each phase.

The student must pass twelve critical tasks: the Army physical fitness test, the combat water survival test, the five-mile run, the eight-mile foot march with full gear, the day and night land navigation tests, the Darby Queen obstacle course, the log walk/rope drop into Victory Pond, the suspension traverse, a 200-foot night rappel or a sixty-foot fixed rope descent in severe weather, eight of twelve knots, and the belay test.

The student must also undergo a peer evaluation at each phase, in which his fellow students rate his leadership qualities and Ranger skills. He must pass at least two of four to graduate. Failure to do so usually results in recycling.

Failure due to medical reasons, classroom and exercise performance, and peer evaluation is not final. The student may retrain at the phase where he failed and continue in the next class.

Students may not recycle if failure is due to negative critical incident (spot) reports or to a negative special observation report (SOR). Spot reports deal with good or bad conduct both in training and in attitude. Spots can be plus or minus, which can cancel each other out. Three minor spots equal one major. Four major minus spots at Fort Benning or three at the other phases are allowed. A cumulative total of five major minus spots results in a review of the student's status. Eight major minus spots mean an automatic dismissal. Students dropped in this manner cannot return to Ranger school.

SORs may also be positive or negative. One negative SOR approved by the brigade chain of command can result in a drop. An SOR as the result of lying, cheating, or stealing means automatic dismissal without chance of reinstatement.

The men who successfully earn their Ranger tabs wear them with pride in the knowledge that they have completed the most physically and mentally grueling training course in the US Army.

Delta Company: Long-Range Surveillance Unit Leaders Course

The 4th Ranger Training Battalion has two companies that do not train Ranger students.

A squad of the Merrills pose with their weapons. The Merrills, part of the 4th Ranger Training Battalion Headquarters and Headquarters Company (HHC), act as the opposing forces for the Darby phase of training. Reinforced, when necessary, by members of the Gulag, the Merrills ambush students on exercises or defend an area under student-led reconnaissance. If discovered or captured, the unfortunate students are held in a prisoner camp until rescued or released.

Rather, they provide specialized training to the rest of the Army. Delta Company conducts a Long-Range Surveillance Unit (LRSU) leaders course at Fort Benning designed to train selected personnel in those technical and operational skills enabling them to train and lead long-range surveillance units in support of corps- and division-level operations.

The course provides training in leadership, physical training, doctrine, organization, and identification of enemy tactics and vehicles. The RIs of Delta Company teach insertion, extraction, communication, and operational techniques. During Desert Storm, Delta Company provided on-the-spot training for the 24th Infantry Division in Saudi Arabia.

The LRSU leaders course is five weeks long. Although previously students had to have a Ranger or Special Forces tab, the expanding needs of the Army have made that requirement obsolete. There are not enough Ranger and Special Forces personnel to meet today's surveillance needs. However, airborne qualification is still required. The course is open to NCOs (sergeant and above) and officers who have been recommended by their units. Specialists 4th class and corporals may be admitted with a waiver.

Part of a squad assumes a defensive stance while listening to the RI during a lesson on patrolling. First, RIs lecture to the students in a classroom setting. Then, the students are walked through the lessons. The lessons are put into practice during field training exercises at Camp Darby, Fort Benning. The patrolling classes were formerly held during the garrison, or Camp Rogers, phase at Fort Benning. Beginning with the class of 1-92 in October 1991, all patrolling instruction takes place at Camp Darby.

Students learn about communications in the first week of training. They are taught to assemble and maintain communication equipment, encoding and decoding, and selecting suitable sites for their transmissions. The week ends with both a written and a hands-on examination. At night, the students bed down in hidden shelters they build.

The second week is devoted to field techniques. The class learns ingress and egress of an area by helicopter and boat. They practice infiltration by rappelling from a helicopter. To exfiltrate, the Special Patrol Insertion & Extraction System (SPIES) is used. Several men are hooked to a special rig on a line and pulled out by helicopter. One man calls it skiing through air. The class also trains in Zodiac boats, learning to approach by water and reconnoiter landing places. Once ashore, the students do a brief reconnaissance and return to the boats. Students must be careful to avoid splashing when entering and exiting the boats so as not to alert opfor trying to ambush students on the way back to the boats.

The students draw weapons and practice battle drills. They learn tracking, counter-tracking, and stalking. They are also introduced to canine operations. Part of the schedule is devoted to LRSU medicine, which is necessary when a unit is isolated in enemy territory. The instruction is similar to that given squad medics in Ranger units.

A squad on patrol at Fort Benning waits for the order to move on. The weight of the rucksack and rifle is usually over seventy pounds. Radiomen and heavy weapons squads carry an even greater weight.

A student company listens to a lecture on patrolling. While the Rangers follow standard infantry doctrine, their execution is more exacting. Staying awake is often a problem, but students are allowed to stand if they feel sleepy. Those who nod off are kept awake by doing push-ups until an RI tells them to return to their seats.

Medics from the 324th Forward Support Battalion treat an injured Ranger student after a jump. The medical bag is in the foreground. The Ranger Training Brigade does not have its own medical support. A medical team from the 324th accompanies each class throughout its training, except to Fort Bliss, which has its own medical battalion.

A Ranger student eats a chocolate cake sandwich. When the students are given hot meals, as opposed to MREs, the food must be eaten on the spot. Anything not finished in the allotted time, usually ten or fifteen minutes, must be returned. If there are seconds, they may not be taken until the first plate is finished. This leads to all sorts of interesting concoctions such as the above sandwich.

The second week ends with hidden shelters and surveillance classes. Students learn how to select sites and build shelters for surveillance and concealment. Usually shallow holes just large enough for three- or six-man teams to lie side-by-side, these hides are camouflaged to conform to the terrain. A team stays in concealment, observing such things as vehicle movement per hour or civilian population densities. The LRSU students spend the nights in hides they build. The hardest lesson learned is the self-discipline and patience required for this type of surveillance.

In the middle of the second week, one day is devoted to remedial training to bring the class up to standard. Any student in danger of failing practices with the help of the RIs those tasks in which the student is deficient. Because of the high caliber of the students, this day is usually regarded as a rest day. The RIs also teach a survival course similar to that given to Ranger students.

The students learn how to breach a wire obstacle by cutting through it. One uses a cutting tool while the other one prepares to thrust the wire aside using a piece of wood or his gloved hand. He has both of their rifles at his side, ready for use if needed. When the breach is wide enough, the cutter will go through and provide covering fire if required. The other student holds the breach open for the rest of the squad to pass through.

The third week is devoted almost entirely to classroom work. The students learn Russian order of battle and tactics. They become familiar with Eastern bloc vehicles and equipment, which are also used by many countries in the Middle East and Asia. This information is necessary in order to relay accurate intelligence from surveillance missions. Using slides and texts developed by the Pentagon and intelligence agencies, the RIs drill students until they can identify enemy equipment even when it is camouflaged. Some of this material is still classified because it may compromise the source.

The dissolution of the Soviet Union has not yet had any effect on this segment of LRSU training. Likely enemies such as Iraq and Libya still use Soviet weapons and tactics. This segment concludes with a written examination. The airborne parachute jump the end of the week is a welcome relief from sitting in a classroom.

The fourth week is spent on situational training exercises such as night insertions and night movement techniques. Patrol bases are established, from which surveillance sites are selected and occupied. Hide sites are built. Each student company conceals a cache of food and draws a map with coordinates indicating the location. The map is then given to another company for later retrieval. This week also ends with an exam.

Field training exercises are conducted in the fifth and final week of LRSU training. The exercises begin with an air assault by helicopter, followed by a SPIES extraction. After an airborne insertion, the exercise continues with movement through the area, surveillance, and evasion of the opfor, played by members of the 4th Ranger Training Battalion headquarters company. Survival tasks are carried out, including recovering the cache of food hidden earlier. If the company looking for the cache cannot find it, they do

An RI shows his students the blank explosives that will simulate grenades during the upcoming exercise. The RIs follow Gen. George S. Patton's dictum, "If you tell it to them dirty, they won't forget it." RIs generally specialize in one or more related skills. During the garrison portion of each phase of training, they teach classes and walk students through exercises. During field exercises, the RIs work twenty-four to forty-eight hours on, and twenty-four hours off. However, paperwork and evaluations cut heavily into off-duty time.

A fire team prepares for an ambush. One student will man the 90mm recoilless rifle, carried by the man on the left, while the other two will cover him and fire at the enemy. The team will not withdraw until the prearranged signal, usually the explosion of captured stores and weapons.

not get any other food. The field training ends with linkups with other units, extraction, and debriefing.

The skills and qualifications of the men who enter the LRSU leaders course ensures a high rate of completion—over ninety percent. Day thirty-five is graduation day.

Echo Company: Infantry Leader Course

Echo Company, 4th Ranger Training Battalion, conducts a training course at Fort Benning, developed by the Ranger Training Brigade for light infantry officers and NCOs to sharpen their skills and enable them to, in turn, train their units to US Army standard. The course also provides an environment which promotes cohesion among a unit's newly appointed leaders. The course length is twenty-eight days with an optimum class size of 118. Each year nine classes are held.

The usual class consists of all the new officers and NCOs of a regiment or division with rank insignia—unlike Ranger school, where rank insignia are not worn. Under the guidance of the RIs, students hone their skills at individual and collective tasks. The instructional process is the same crawl/walk/run method used throughout the training battalion.

An RI walks a student through a bowline knot. The RI will continue to work with the student until the knot is learned. Knot tieing is one of the critical tasks necessary to earn the Ranger tab.

Students at Camp Frank D. Merrill, Dahlonega, Georgia, learn to use the rappelling rope to belay—stop. The technique is important for safety on the mountains.

A Ranger on patrol covers a section of road while other members of his squad cross.

The commander of the 5th Ranger Training Battalion prepares to jump with his students. Battalion commanders are encouraged to spend time in the field evaluating students. Of course, commanders are delighted to leave their desks.

A Ranger student practices the Australian, or forward-facing rappel. Notice his gloved hands on the rappelling line ready to belay (stop) or slow his descent. The line passes through a snaplink on his belt. The wooden slat wall, which is approximately twenty feet high, descends to a dirt pit that cushions any falls.

A Ranger student rappels with full pack down a sixty-foot cliff. His right hand is positioned to slow or stop his descent. Students must perform three daytime rappels: one with rucksack, one without rucksack, and one using only two bounces against the cliff wall while descending. The rappel with rucksack at night is one of the critical tasks needed for graduation. Gloves protect the hands while rappelling. The number on his helmet is assigned at the beginning of the class at Fort Benning. By the mountain phase, there are far fewer than 286 students in the class. The mountaineering phase of Ranger training results in the most injuries and medical recycles, especially in winter, when the cliff face can become a sheet of ice.

The MRE, Meal Ready to Eat, is the staple of Ranger training. During field exercises, one MRE per day is usually the only food provided. It comes in a compact foil pouch, can be heated or eaten cold, and provides 3,000 calories. If the MRE is heated in boiling water, the water must be discarded afterward because toxic chemicals leach out of the wrapping. The kindest thing the men say is that an MRE won't hurt your ribs if you fall on it while landing in a drop zone.

A Ranger student learns how to carry his injured buddy down a cliff. Number 279 [the b/w photo] is the "injured" one. The rope around his body secures him to the line. The rescuer can easily lose his balance while rappelling. Fortunately, the student above recovered and completed the descent safely. RIs threaten to assign the smallest students to carry the heaviest ones. This threat is rarely carried out.

An "enemy" patrols at Camp Merrill, watching for a student raid. The opfors are made up of Rangers from the headquarters company who stay in the field during the entire exercise. Opfors wear older uniforms such as this World War II German officer's cap. The weapons are captured Eastern bloc equipment or reasonable facsimiles. Sometimes opfor uniforms are improvised by turning the standard uniform inside out.

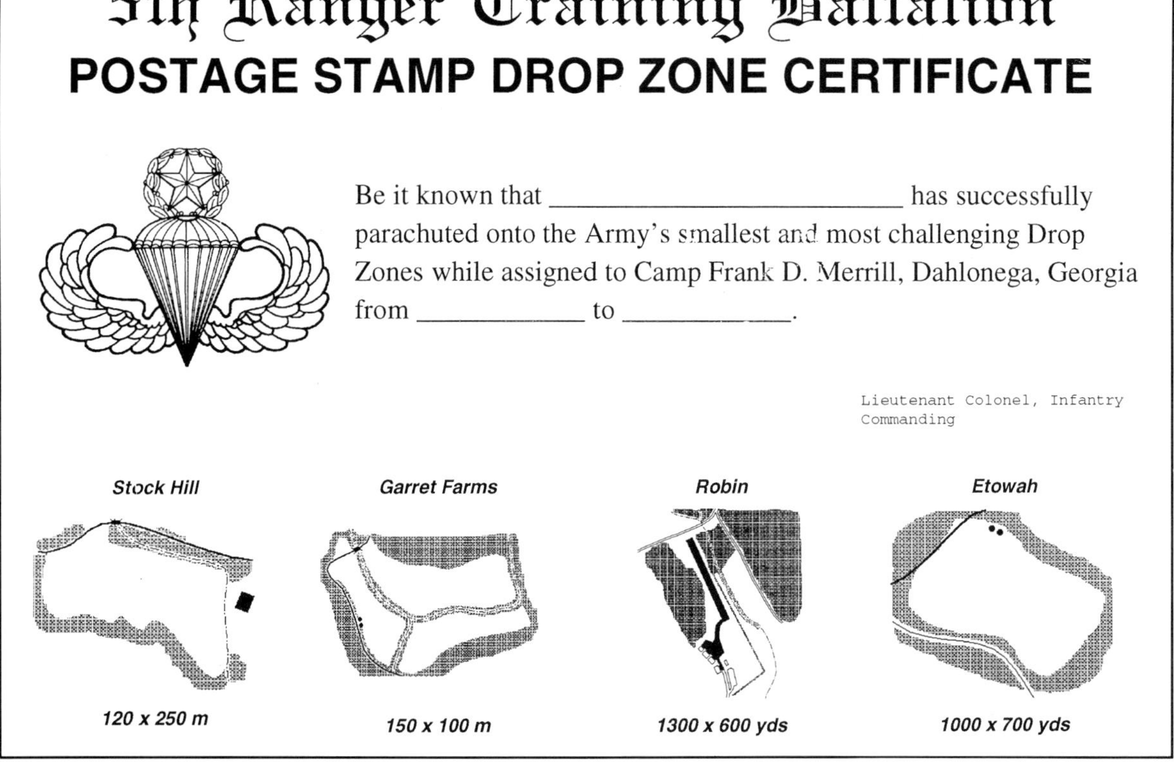
5th Ranger Training Battalion
POSTAGE STAMP DROP ZONE CERTIFICATE

Be it known that ______________________ has successfully parachuted onto the Army's smallest and most challenging Drop Zones while assigned to Camp Frank D. Merrill, Dahlonega, Georgia from ____________ to ____________.

Lieutenant Colonel, Infantry
Commanding

The certificate given to RIs when they first jump into the drop zones at Camp Merrill. The students usually jump into Garret Farms, the smallest.

The students retrain in individual skills such as issuing orders in the proper form and coordinating with adjacent units. They conduct leader's reconnaissance and analyze terrain. Many tasks are map-related: navigating, locating targets, and orienting indirect fire. The leaders also learn how to conduct training to standard for these tasks in their units.

They go on to collective tasks (carried out by more than one individual) that are necessary for small unit, light infantry missions. They practice attacks, raids, ambushes, and movement to contact. They train in reconnaissance and security procedures. They practice reacting to combat, breaking off contact, reacting to indirect fire. They conduct platoon attack drills and critique their actions. Some of the men have not performed any battle drills since their basic training. They must regain their own skills before they can expect to train their unit. The drills also afford an opportunity to observe the abilities of their fellows. Unlike Ranger school, food and sleep are adequate.

The last two weeks of the course consist of situational and field training exercises. Typically, a situational excercise will involve an attack on one of the objectives at Camp Darby, often Cin-

A Ranger student in a patrol base at Camp Merrill takes the opportunity to eat and attend to personal hygiene. A patrol base is usually located in areas near missions. However, it should be away from any area of value. This means that it is usually in uncomfortable and inhospitable spots. This patrol base can be reached only by climbing over a narrow ridge and down a steep slope. If opfors catch students in a patrol base, the base has to be moved and the platoon sergeant and platoon leader may receive a no-go for the exercise. After a mission, students still have to watch out for an ambush on the way back to base. Students spend the nights in the patrol bases for the duration of the mission.

A student who tangled his rifle in the lines of his main parachute deploys his reserve chute as a safety measure.

A jumper prepares to land near the smoke marking the drop zone. He has to avoid the trees all around him.

SPIES is used to extract an LRSU team. It is used to quickly remove three or four men from an area.

Black Hawks deliver students to a landing zone high in the mountains of North Georgia. They will have to survive the attack by the opfor and then continue on to their patrol base.

An RI at Camp Rudder, Eglin Air Force Base, Florida, shows a student how to secure the rope for a stream crossing. Rope bridges and stream crossings are now taught only at Fort Benning and at Camp Merrill.

derblock Village. The village and its surrounding bunkers are manned by Rangers from 4th Ranger Training Battalion headquarters company and members of the Gulag. The RIs of Echo Company observe the action. The leaders have to move toward the village, often crossing enemy lines and fighting if necessary. If there is contact with an opfor, the RIs receive an immediate after-action report, complete with casualty figures and ammunition expended.

The platoon and company leaders send out reconnaissance squads to the objective and then determine where to place their fire teams. If ladders for scaling or any such equipment is needed, they are built at this point. If artillery support is requested, the mission leader calls for it. Then comes the attack on the objective, which

A student crosses a stream by hauling himself along the safety rope. Once on the other side, he will join his squad to carry out the rest of the mission. If he is fortunate, he will be able to change into dry clothes before he beds down for the night. Even when a student is not in the water, he is always wet at Camp Rudder—hot and wet in summer, cold and wet in winter. The high humidity and swampy ground afford little opportunity for drying out. The major medical danger in this environment is the constant threat of cellulitus. Hallucinations, especially about food, are not uncommon by the Florida phase. One student "saw" giant pizzas rolling along the ground. Students mistake bushes for their buddies. One student sleepwalked to the RIs' campfire and tried to attack the "enemy force." When he was awakened, he had no idea where he was or how he got there.

should be within a time specified by the operations order.

Things usually do not go smoothly in the early exercises. One group made so much noise trying to build scaling ladders, the defenders in the village could hear them coming almost an hour before the attack. One group couldn't find the village until two hours after the scheduled time for the assault. One hungry defender who had missed lunch joked he was going to find the attackers himself and show them the way. Sometimes, the attackers call down artillery on their own positions, knocking off most of their forces. The later exercises are more efficient.

After the battle, the final after-action report is given. An exercise that results in more than ten percent casualties is considered unsuccessful, even if the objective is taken. Unlike Ranger school, these exercises are not graded, only critiqued. The RIs guide the group in criticizing the action and making suggestions for improvements.

Field training exercises are conducted under combat conditions, but without live fire. Platoons usually participate as part of a larger unit. The field training exercises, using Military Integrated Laser Engagement System (MILES), involves movement to contact and raids, ambushes, and reconnaissance. A field training exercise usually

An RI in the prow of the Zodiac boat directs a squad of students along a river. Even on a trial run, the students carry full gear and wear camouflage paint. By this time, the original class of 300 students has dwindled to about 100. The three companies have become three platoons.

begins with helicopter movement to a landing zone a few miles from the first objective. The company moves through enemy territory, reacting to contact when necessary. They then establish and occupy an operational rally point (ORP), from which they set up an ambush. After the ambush, the company regroups and gives an after-action report to the observing RIs. Afterward, the company moves on to establish a patrol base where the men spend what is left of the night.

The next day, the company crosses a dangerous area where they are subject to indirect fire. Once past this area, they are resupplied by air and move to an ORP near their final objective. From there, the company reconnoiters the objective. The objective is then raided with the aid of fire support. After another after-action report, the company moves out to an area from which they are flown or trucked back to camp. The exercise ends with a final after-action report. The RIs

A student waits for the rest of his squad before proceeding deeper into the swamp.

A student studies the radio equipment Long-Range Surveillance Unit (LRSU) teams use in the field. He must be able to assemble and disassemble the radio rapidly.

An RI instructs an LRSU team in how to infiltrate by water. The boat is a zodiac.

An LRSU student crawls inland for a brief reconnaissance.

UNITED STA

An RI checks out the exit door before takeoff.

LRSUs are often inserted into an area by rappelling from helicopters. This Black Hawk is inserting a team at Camp Darby.

and leaders analyze the exercise and comment on performance.

At the end of the course, students know more about the abilities of their fellow officers and NCOs. They have sharpened their own skills and are ready for the task of training their unit. The Rangers call the process "rebluing."

Echo Company: DEA Training Program

Echo Company conducts another training program that is not very well known. Agents chosen by the US Drug Enforcement Agency (DEA) are trained at Fort Benning to combat the drug trade in the jungles of South America. The eight-week program includes physical training, weapons training, and jungle and mountain training. The course is modified from the Ranger Training Course to suit the needs of the DEA agents. There is no sleep or food deprivation. Agents train in the sort of clothing they wear on the job, mostly t-shirts and camouflage pants.

The agents learn how to locate and raid a cocaine laboratory and return safely to base. To facilitate training, the Rangers have their own "lab" complete with fierce "drug dealers" to fight off the gringos. The men of Echo Company make most convincing enemies. Captured weapons and equipment are used to add to the realism. Only the cocaine is fake.

Part of the training is also conducted on-site in the mountains of Peru and Bolivia. There, the Rangers also provide training for the local forces as part of Operation Snow Cap. Camps and patrol bases are set up and used as in combat. The war on drugs is as real as any other war.

Members of the 10th Mountain Division run to board a Black Hawk while it is still in motion.

A defender in Cinderblock Village fires his M60 at the attackers. Note the Military Integrated Laser Engagement System (MILES) on the barrel. The defender is a member of the Gulag at Fort Benning. He will join the next Ranger school class as soon as he is medically fit. Meanwhile, he helps out by acting as part of the defending force for training exercises.

A student in the infantry leaders course rushes through the gate of Cinderblock Village during an assault. The smoke helps to conceal the attackers. The smoke can also act as a code for those in the rear: red smoke for danger, green smoke for clear.

Members of the Gulag at Fort Benning climb a tower at Cinderblock Village before an attack by the 10th Mountain Division members at the infantry leaders course.

Army Black Hawk helicopters at Camp Darby.

Students rapidly exit the Black Hawk and take cover.

The honor graduates are presented with their awards at a Ranger school graduation ceremony.

The new Rangers rush off the field after graduation ceremonies end. Most of them will rush right to the nearest restaurant. Some men report that after the end of the Ranger course, they had cravings for all sorts of food. For a few months, one student couldn't pass a convenience store without buying candy bars.

Friends and family pin the hard-earned Ranger tab on the graduates.

Chapter 3

75th Ranger Regiment

Activation of 75th Ranger Regiment

The 1st Battalion (Ranger), 75th Infantry, was officially activated 8 February 1974 at Fort Stewart, Georgia, after training at Fort Benning. Its headquarters was at Hunter Army Airfield, Georgia. The 2nd Battallion (Ranger), 75th Infantry, was activated 1 October 1974 at Fort Lewis, Washington. The 3rd Battalion (Ranger), 75th Infantry, and Headquarters and Headquarters Company (Ranger), 75th Infantry, were activated 3 October 1984 at Fort Benning, Georgia. Subsequently, the three battalions and the headquarters and headquarters company were redesignated as the 75th Ranger Regiment. This was the first time that an organization of this size was officially recognized as the parent headquarters of the Ranger battalions. Not since Darby's Ranger Force headquarters has the US Army had such a large Ranger force—over 2,000 men.

Mission

The 75th Ranger Regiment is the nation's premier strike force, able to move across any terrain and endure any hardship necessary to complete its mission. It provides the United States the ability to move a credible military force to any region of the world in eighteen hours. Its ability to perform both light infantry tasks and special operations allows it to plan and conduct special forces missions as well as light infantry operations assigned to airborne, air assault, and light infantry battalions.

The Rangers can be deployed quickly to all types of terrain and weather conditions, infiltrating and assaulting by land, sea, and air. They conduct strike operations, including raids, interdictions, and personnel and equipment recovery. Ranger units perform specialized light infantry missions such as securing airfields, and destroying communications centers and command and control facilities. They also conduct short-duration reconnaissance. Ranger units usually operate three days in the field without resupply. Longer missions require resupply by whatever methods available. Limited operations are possible under nuclear, biological, or chemical warfare conditions.

Rangers can carry out quick-response operations such as they did in Grenada, or deliberate long-planned operations as in the case of Panama. In either case, Rangers are used in situations that require their unique skills. They should not be used for missions that can be accomplished by conventional forces.

The 75th Ranger Regiment fights as a light infantry force, following infantry doctrine and rules of operations, with special emphasis on METT-T factors. The typical Ranger mission requires initiative, depth, agility, and synchronization above that usually found in light infantry units. Detailed planning and coordination are most important to exploit the enemy's weakness and avoid his strengths. Rangers hold premission training briefings and rehearsals using all equipment and personnel needed for the actual mission. Individ-

Grant of Arms

By authority of the Secretary of the Army, The Institute of Heraldry, United States Army, gives, grants and assigns unto the 75th Ranger Regiment, the arms following:

Blazon

Shield: Quarterly azure and vert, between the first and fourth quarters a radiant sun of twelve points and a mullet argent, a lightning flash coupled bendinisterwise gules fimbriated or.

Crest: On a wreath of the colors argent and azure, issuing in back of an embattlement of a tower with six merlons or a pedestal gules supporting a clinthe affronte of the third in front of a torteau within an annulet of the second.

Motto: Sua Sponte (of their own accord). The original Marauders, like today's Rangers, were all volunteers.

Symbolism

The colors blue, white, red, and green represent four of the original six combat teams of the 5307th Composite Unit (Provisional), commonly referred to as "Merrill's Marauders," which were identified by color. To avoid confusion, the other two colors, khaki and orange, were not represented in the design; however, khaki was represented by the color of the uniform worn by US forces in the China-Burma-India Theater during World War II. The unit's close cooperation with the Chinese forces in the China-Burma-India Theater is represented by the sun symbol from the Chinese flag. The white star represents the Star of Burma, the country in which the Marauders campaigned during World War II. The lightning bolt is symbolic of the strike characteristics of the Marauders' behind-the-line-activities.

Crest: The organization's service in the China-Burma-India Theater of World War II is represented by the clinthe (a gold Burmese lion). The blue annulet symbolized the Presidential Unit Citation awarded for service at Myitkyina, Burma, the "gateway to China." The gold embattlement in base refers to the unit's combat services in Vietnam while the six merlons represent six Valorous Unit awards; the two Meritorious Unit Commendations earned by elements of the Regiment are denoted by the scarlet disc at center.

Rangers Lead The Way

ual and unit initiative are encouraged to take advantage of changing battlefield conditions.

Surprise is a hallmark of Ranger missions. Operations conducted at night and during poor weather conditions tend to throw an enemy force off balance. Different methods of insertion and attack help prevent the enemy from discovering a pattern of operation. Deception, including using concurrent military operations as cover, and a willingness to accept risk to confuse the enemy are standard procedures. Coupled with the mobility, speed, and violence of execution, the shock effect of surprise often allows the Ranger unit to complete the mission before the enemy can react.

Using the normal infantry techniques of stealth and concealment, Rangers enhance their survivability. Taking full advantage of terrain allows Rangers to determine the time and place of combat. Rapidly departing the area by a different route after the mission is completed also helps keep casualties down.

The lack of organic combat support limits Ranger units to whatever support is available in the theater of operations. Limited air defense weapons and indirect fire support, and the lack of casualty evacuation capability, can further restrict the use of Rangers. However, the need to train replacements rather than simply reassign troops from other units is the most limiting factor of Ranger unit operations.

Organization

The 75th Ranger Regiment consists of three battalions, headquarters, and a headquarters company: 1st Battalion is located at Hunter Army Air Field, Georgia; 2nd Battalion at Fort Lewis, Washington; and 3rd Battalion at Fort Benning, Georgia. Regimental headquarters, also at Fort Benning, consists of the commander (a colonel) and his staff and contains five sections: personnel (S-1), intelligence (S-2), operations and training (S-3), supply (S-4), and civil affairs (S-5). The regimental commander also has a special staff that includes a communications officer, fire support officer, surgeon, and a staff judge advocate. A weather officer from the US Air Force and a tactical air control officer are also permanently assigned.

The regimental headquarters company consists of the company commander and his staff, including company S-1, S-2, S-3, S-4, and S-5, similar to headquarters. The headquarters company also contains the fire support element, communications platoon, reconnaissance platoon, medical treatment team, and the Ranger Indoctrination Program (RIP), which processes new recruits. Headquarters company provides support to the battalions when needed.

Each battalion consists of three combat companies and a battalion Headquarters and Headquarters Company (HHC). The battalion HHC

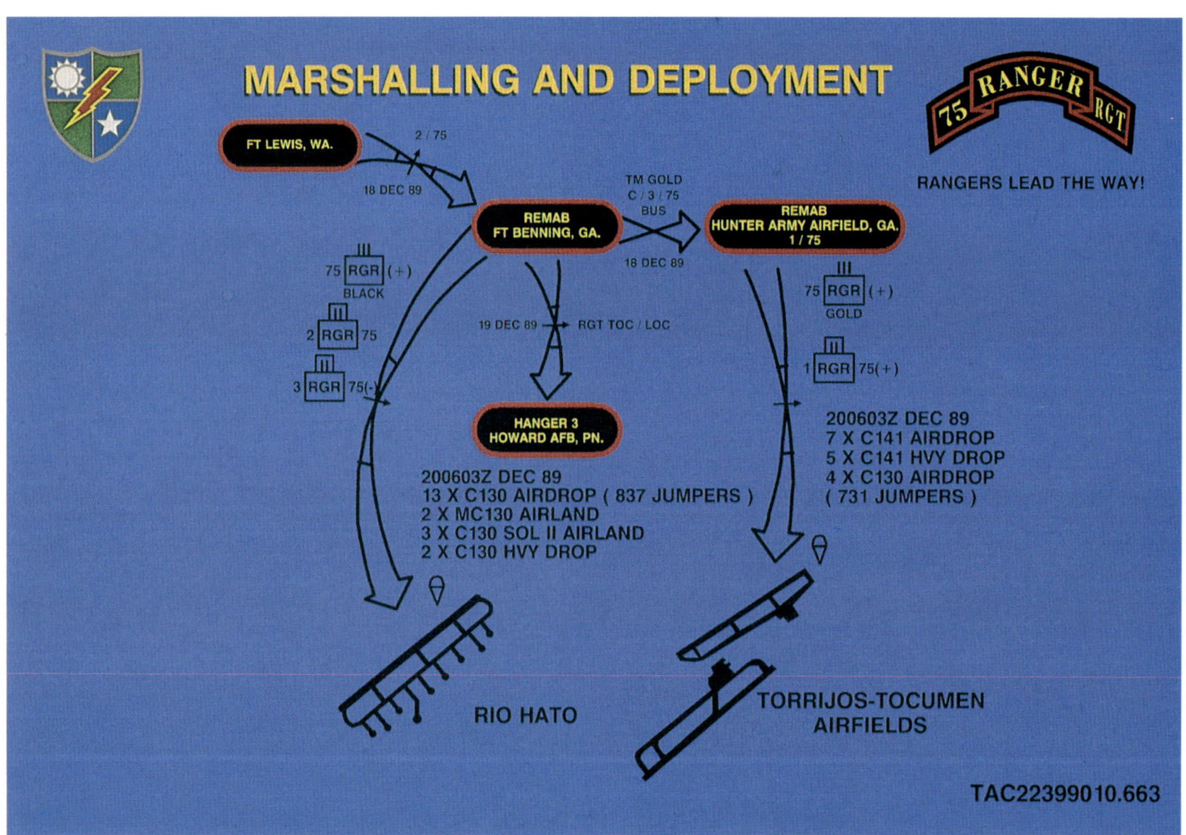

Deploying Ranger units. (RSE is Ranger Support Element, TOC is Tactical Operations Command, LOC is Logistical Operations Command, CONUS is Continental United States.) Ranger units can be deployed anywhere in the world in eighteen hours. One Ranger battalion is always on call as the Ranger Ready Force, with weapons and equipment packed for quick loading onto transports. US Army includes company headquarters, a fire support team, the medical team, the communications team, and a support section that includes food service.

Ranger companies are heavy companies with three rifle platoons of about forty-five men each, and a weapons platoon of half that size. The rifle platoons are made up of three rifle squads of three teams each and a machine gun squad. All squad leaders are at least staff sergeants and team leaders are sergeants. Specialists—equivalent to corporals—who have the Ranger tab may also be team leaders when necessary. The heavy concentration of NCOs in Ranger companies allows a

Members of the pre-Ranger course at Fort Benning prepare for the dinner break. Although the course is designed to prepare the men of the 75th for the Ranger school, there is no sleep or food deprivation. The men must be in top physical shape when they enter Ranger school.

A fire team from B Company, 3/75, checks out its surroundings on the way to a raid. The Rangers practice with MILES for live-fire exercises held throughout the year.

Men of the 3/75 move rapidly through a wooded area. Rangers must be fit enough to cover ground quickly, carrying everything they need. The total weight of weapons and supplies can be over 100lb per man. The Ranger Regiment is the only unit in the Army to mandate physical training five days a week, forty-eight weeks a year.

A squad from the 3/75 halts before moving on patrol. The squad is positioned to cover each other as well as the area. As a result of countless training drills, the men take the correct positions automatically.

Members of the 75th Ranger Regiment Headquarters Company Reconnaissance platoon with communications equipment. The platoon contains three teams that infiltrate enemy territory and remain on patrol for up to five days before returning. Using observation and electronic and photographic devices, the teams collect as much information as possible. The platoon's findings are reported by secure, long-range communications before the teams exfiltrate. The platoon operates for the regiment or for the battalions. US Army

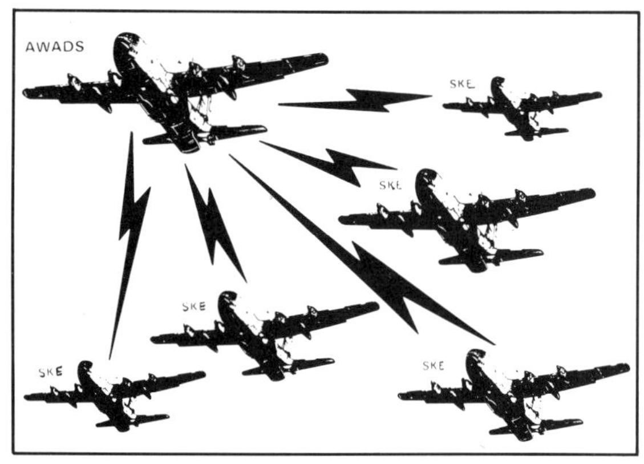

Adverse Weather Aerial Delivery Systems (AWADS) and Station Keeping Equipment (SKE) aircraft formation. C-130s equipped with AWADS allow Rangers to make airborne insertions in virtually any kind of weather. The system uses a Doppler radar that calculates the ground speed of the aircraft and an AWADS computer programmed with flight route information, such as direction, airspeed, and route, to show where the aircraft is in relation to programmed checkpoints. Only a few C-130s have an AWADS aboard. The rest of the flight have SKE that tells the crew where the aircraft is in relation to the others in the formation. The two systems combine to allow Rangers to jump in poor visibility when an enemy force cannot track them. US Army great amount of individual initiative without sacrificing the level of performance. Ranger units also have the highest percentage of NCOs who later become officers in the Army.

Although Ranger units have no casualty evacuation capability, they can provide medical care in the field. All team, squad, and platoon leaders learn basic first aid and how to administer intravenous injections to prevent shock. Each squad has a medic who received emergency medical treatment training provided by the regiment. When necessary, they assist the platoon medics; otherwise, the squad medics carry a rifle.

The battalions rotate as the Ranger Ready Force. For one month the designated battalion must be ready to deploy anywhere in the world within eighteen hours. This means that supplies and ammunition must be secured on pallets ready

"The guards at a South American jungle drug lab lounge around, waiting for the cocaine to be trucked out." In reality, men of B Company are acting as the opfor for C Company, 3/75, during a rehearsal of a drug raid. The exercise, which will be evaluated, will take place the next night. The men of the 75th often train against each other; both sides benefit from acting against opposition.

Behind a cloud of smoke, the raid begins. Note the MILES on the webbing of the men.

Two of the bad guys use the fallen branches as cover to attack a raider. The oncoming Ranger moves from tree to tree toward the drug lab.

A squad in the pre-Ranger course emerges from the woods at the end of the day. The v-shaped formation, which allows the men to cover each other, marks them as Rangers who carry out every small training detail as if in combat.

for loading onto transports. The battalion must be able to recall its men from leave and assemble in a few hours prepared for combat. A longer period on alert tends to degrade the performance of the unit.

Recruitment and Training

Rangers say they volunteer four times in their careers: to join the Army, to go to airborne school, to join the Ranger Regiment, and to go to Ranger school. All Rangers in the 75th ("scroll" Rangers), officers and enlisted, are recruited from airborne units. The men who wear the 75th unit scroll insignia say that the Ranger Tab is a school. The scroll is a way of life.

Rangers are expected to train to standard and beyond. While their battle drills are common to all light infantry, Rangers perform them with an extra edge. They never let up. Every drill, every exercise, every alert is conducted as though they were in combat. Even returning to the barracks after days in the field, a Ranger unit will move in the combat V-formation. Such actions became instinctive.

Occasionally, training is more relaxed, as in a Hollywood jump where full uniform and equipment are not used. In those circumstances, while the clothing is not regulation, the procedure is. They may joke before and after, but during the parachute jump everything goes by the book.

All Rangers in a unit are expected to know the details of a mission so that if a squad, platoon, or company leader is put out of action, someone else can take over without loss of efficiency. Such rigorous training requires a great deal of self-discipline, but produces a confident soldier who can be permitted to use his initiative when needed.

Most Rangers do not spend their entire Army careers in the 75th Regiment. Some go on to the Ranger Training Brigade for a tour of duty and then return to the 75th for another tour. Only a handful manage to serve their entire careers in Ranger units. Often, Rangers of every rank find it difficult to adjust to other types of units. They find the training and discipline too easy. As one sergeant put it, "In the Rangers, the hours are lousy, but the action's great."

All enlisted recruits undergo a three-and-one-

A dead bad guy lies near the makeshift lab. The folded arms and crossed legs indicate the body has been searched. Those who are "killed" during a rehearsal are predetermined. The actual exercise will be more realistic.

half-week training program (RIP), designed to eliminate the weak or nonmotivated. Within a stressful environment, the new recruits must pass the physical training, operations, and procedures tests. In addition to passing the standard Army physical fitness tests, the recruits must complete an eight-kilometer run in forty minutes, and a twelve-kilometer road march with full rucksack and weapons. Recruits also must complete six-, eight-, and twelve-kilometer road marches with increasing rates of speed.

The recruits must pass day and night navigation tests and show their familiarity with the battle drills and procedures necessary to a member of a light infantry squad. Three jumps are conducted, with a tactical mission immediately following the last jump, which is a night jump.

Throughout RIP, Ranger lineage, history, and traditions are taught. The attrition rate varies according to weather and time of year, but averages about forty percent. Those who fail but show willingness and have the right attitude are allowed to try again.

After RIP, the new Rangers go to the battalions for operational training. The normal tour of duty is three years. Within six to twelve months, those who wish to earn the Ranger tab go to the Ranger school. With the exception of clerical staff,

A Ranger wearing a camouflaged helmet guards the perimeter of the area after the raid. The camouflage on the helmet is made up of strips torn from a uniform.

A team searches the perimeter. Rangers always *work in pairs, ever since the days of Darby.*

cooks, and others in similar positions, those Rangers who want to be promoted to specialist and NCO must earn the Ranger tab. Entry in Ranger school is based on order of merit, seniority, and the number of places available. A clerk at 75th headquarters is one of only five clerks in the Army with the tab.

Those who go to Ranger school attend the pre-Ranger course one month before the start of their Ranger school class. Given by the RIP cadre at Fort Benning, the pre-Ranger course prepares the men for Ranger school by training and testing on the basics of Ranger skills such as raids, reconnaissance, patrols, and ambushes. Physical training requirements are reviewed. To prevent physical deterioration before Ranger school, the men are not deprived of sleep and food. The program gives battalion Rangers a head start. Their attrition rate in Ranger school is less than ten percent.

All officers and NCOs recruited for the 75th must be graduates of Ranger school and airborne-qualified. Officers must have served at least one year in a leadership position in a non-Ranger unit. This means that an officer must be at least a first lieutenant before joining the Rangers. There are no inexperienced leaders in the regiment.

Officers and NCOs go through the Ranger Orientation Program before reporting to the battalions. In a nonstress environment they undergo the Army Physical Fitness Test and complete a five-mile run.

Ranger units have the most intense training schedule in the Army—forty-eight weeks a year. They train under tough, stressful, and often hazardous conditions, including live fire—as close to actual combat as possible. Field training exercises often set one unit against another, increasing the competitiveness of both. The opfor tries to be as authentic as possible. Often, an exercise will be repeated until each unit has played both sides.

All training is performance oriented. The level of proficiency is important, not the number of hours required. If a standard calls for certain hours of training, Rangers will do more if required. If proficiency is attained sooner, the unit goes on to other tasks. To this end, exercises are often evaluated and rated. These exercises are planned and rehearsed as if they were actual missions. Rehearsals are conducted during the day. However, most exercises are performed in darkness, as are most Ranger missions. Training is also conducted with other units at the Joint Readiness Training Center in Arkansas.

Each battalion holds a readiness exercise once or twice a year. Without prior preparation, the battalion must assemble men and equipment for immediate movement. Then, just as in actual combat, they are loaded into C-130s or other transport for a parachute jump into the target area. These exercises are usually graded for speed and efficiency. One must not be sacrificed for the other. These exercises are independent of the Ranger Ready Force rotation.

Rangers train in environments as close to real combat missions as possible. During a three-year

The raiders give an ACE report to their team leader, who will pass it along to the squad and platoon leaders. The report details the amount of ammunition expended, the casualties suffered, and the equipment captured or destroyed.

Cadre of the 4th Ranger Training Battalion board the OV-10 for a jump. Two or three jumpers and a jumpmaster fit in each OV-10.

Rangers inspect the OV-10 Bronco that will drop them for a practice jump.

period, each battalion trains at least twice in extreme cold and in amphibious operations. Jungle, mountain, and desert training are done at least once every year. Urban training is undergone every six months. Such environmental training includes critical skills and techniques necessary to each area.

Throughout the training cycle, physical training is not neglected. Rangers conduct physical training, including runs at a pace of at least one mile in eight minutes, five days a week. All other Army units usually conduct physical training one or two days in seven.

The results of this intensive and lengthy training schedule provide the finest light infantry regiment in the US armed forces, perhaps in the world.

Members of C Company, 1/75, in a desert training exercise in the United States. The Rangers train in a desert environment at least once a year. US Army via Col. David Grange

A Navy Ch-47 carries Rangers of the 3/75 for a water jump into Lake Eufala, Alabama. The jump is a "Hollywood" one; that is, it is not done with full uniform and gear.

The jumpers slide out the back as the OV-10 pitches near vertical, but the jumpmaster stays in the aircraft.

The jump into Lake Eufala. The men inflate their life vests as a safety measure before they hit the water. In case of a problem, the wet parachute would drag them under before they could use the life vest.

As part of the safety orientation, a Ranger learns how to extricate himself from a tangled parachute.

Capt. Chae, Col. David Grange, CW3 "Doc" Donovan (left to right) at Dekkar Airstrip, Fort Benning, during a Mangudai officers training exercise, November 1991. Mangudais usually begin with an air assault or jump, followed by a patrol. The officers of the 75th train as hard and as often as their men. US Army via Col. David Grange

75th Regimental officers on a run at Fort Benning, September 1991, following a three-day tactical training exercise with no food or sleep. Code-named Mangudai, the exercise provides periodic stress training for the 75th's officers. When in physical training uniforms, Rangers wear running shoes. US Army via Col. David Grange

The Ranger Creed

R Recognizing that I volunteered as a Ranger, fully knowing the hazards of my chosen profession, I will always endeavor to uphold the prestige, honor, and high "esprit de corps" of the Ranger Regiment.

A Acknowledging the fact that a Ranger is a more elite soldier who arrives at the cutting edge of a battle by land, sea, or air, I accept the fact that as a Ranger, my country expects me to move farther, faster, and fight harder than any other soldier.

N Never shall I fail my comrades. I will always keep myself mentally alert, physically strong, and morally straight and I will shoulder more than my share of the task, whatever it may be. One hundred percent and then some.

G Gallantly will I show the world that I am a specially selected and well-trained soldier. My courtesy to superiors, my neatness of dress, and my care of equipment shall set the example for others to follow.

E Energetically will I meet the enemies of my country. I shall defeat them on the field of battle, for I am better trained and will fight with all my might. Surrender is not a Ranger word. I will never leave a fallen comrade to fall into the hands of the enemy and under no circumstances will I ever embarrass my country.

R Readily will I display the intestinal fortitude required to fight on to the Ranger objective and complete the mission, though I be the lone survivor.

RANGERS LEAD THE WAY

Chapter 4

Weapons and Equipment

Each Ranger battalion is supplied with the latest light infantry weapons and equipment. These include laser range finders, infrared aiming devices, and all types of night vision aids. However, the Rangers will use whatever is effective for them, even if it is not the most up-to-date. They still use the 90mm recoilless rifle and are one of the last units to do so.

The Rangers can also call on support from other units throughout the armed forces. The Air Force Special Operations Command at Hurlburt Field, Eglin Air Force Base, Florida, supplies specialized transports such as the MC-130 Talons and helicopters when needed.

The Navy provides transport and fire support when asked. During Urgent Fury, the Navy provided helicopters for evacuation and fire support. Throughout the Vietnam War, Navy units provided boats for river ambushes. Ranger units often called on Navy gunners to cover an extraction from areas near the coasts.

Of course, the Army provides the majority of support to the 75th: most transport, indirect fire, antiaircraft fire, and other combat support. Medics to work with the Ranger Training Brigade come from the 324th Forward Support Battalion at Fort Benning and from units at Fort Bliss.

As light infantry, Rangers are issued all standard Army uniforms and equipment. Special equipment such as sniper rifles is used by those Rangers who have additional training. Only twenty-four such rifles are issued to each battalion. The basic weapon is still the M16.

Rangers tie items such as canteens and knives to their webbing so they can grab their rifles without losing time or equipment.

An M67 90mm recoilless rifle. Not all the equipment used by the Rangers is up-to-date. If something has proved its worth, it is used until a better replacement comes along. The Rangers are virtually the only unit in the US military to still use the 90mm.

The Military Integrated Laser Engagement System, or MILES, is used with M16s and M60s. One part fits on the front of the gun barrel, and the other part is worn by the Ranger. When the gun fires a blank, the laser is activated. If the gun is aimed correctly, the receiver on the target beeps. More than one hit, the target is considered killed. The MILES is a valuable tool, but in deep foliage or heavy fog, the system will not work accurately. Of course, if the batteries run out, the system doesn't work anywhere.

An M60 machine gun, the type used throughout the infantry.

An AN/PVS-4 night vision individual weapons sight. A second-generation starlight system, it may also be handheld for night observation. It mounts on the M14 and M16 rifles, M60 machine gun, M67 recoilless rifle, M72A2 Light Antitank Weapon, and the M79 grenade launcher. Its range is 600 meters in moonlight and 300 meters in starlight.

A Ranger simulates the arming of an M18A1 claymore mine. Such mines can be set off by trip wires or remotely and are very useful in laying ambushes.

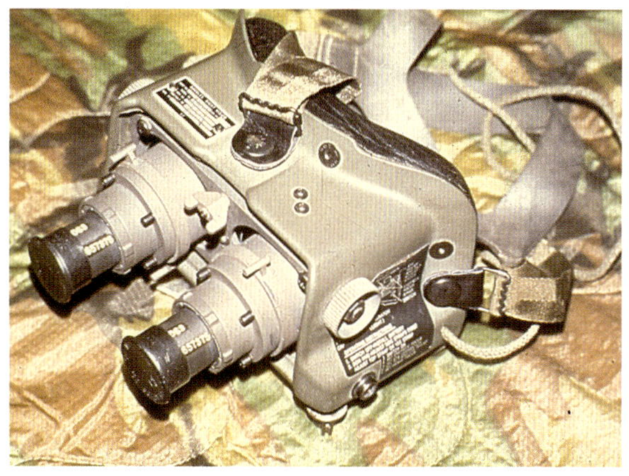

These AN/PVS-5 night vision goggles are lightweight and battery powered with a built-in infrared source for close-up viewing. They provide a forty-degree field of view with a range of 150 meters in moonlight and fifty meters in starlight, sufficient to spot a man-sized target at those distances. US Army

The latest version AN/PVS-7B night vision goggles provide improved night vision in lower light levels. The range is the same as the AN/PVS-5. Most of the Ranger missions take place at least part of the time in darkness, so such night vision devices allow them to move freely.

A Ranger manually inflates his B-7 life vest. The vest is standard equipment on any mission involving water other than stream crossings.

A Ranger holds an M16 rifle, the basic weapon of the US Army.

Previous page
An MC-130E Combat Talon II from the 8th Special Operations Squadron, 1st Special Operations Wing, Hurlburt Field, Florida. Like the Talon I, the Talon II is a Lockheed C-130E modified for special operations support. The electronics have been upgraded so that it is even more effective. The Talon II does not have the STAR yoke. It was determined that the STAR system would be more effective on helicopters.

An MC-130E Combat Talon from the 8th Special Operations Squadron, 1st Special Operations Wing, Hurlburt Field, Florida. The specialized aerial delivery equipment on the MC-130 enables it to locate small drop zones and make high-speed deliveries with great accuracy day or night into unfamiliar terrain. At fifty feet or above, the Talon can deliver personnel at 144mph, and equipment at 150 to 288mph. The yoke on the nose is the Fulton Surface-to-Air Recovery (STAR) system, which can recover two people or a 500lb package in less than ten minutes from land or water.

An MH-53J Pave Low helicopter from the 1st Special Operations Wing, Hurlburt Field, Florida. A version of the H-53, the Pave Low is considered the most sophisticated helicopter in the West. It has either three 7.62mm mini-guns or three .50ca machine guns and armor plating. It has a range of 600 miles and is capable of air refueling. The crew of six can carry thirty-seven passengers or 13,000lb of cargo. It can be used as an air ambulance, holding sixteen litters and four medical attendants. The electronics include the forward-looking infrared receiver (FLIR) for night vision, terrain following and mapping radar, Doppler radar for navigation, and a mission computer. Its electronic and infrared countermeasure systems make it a formidable support helicopter for special operations missions.

Previous page
An AH-64 Apache helicopter in flight. The Apache provides fire support with its advanced sighting and fire control systems. It has a 30mm chain gun automatic cannon under the fuselage and carries rockets or Hellfire missiles.

An AC-130H gunship from the 8th Special Operations Squadron, 1st Special Operations Wing, Hurlburt Field, Florida. The gunships provide fire support during jumps and landings into enemy areas.

Close-up of guns on an AC-130H gunship. Armament includes two 20mm Vulcan cannons, one 40mm Bofors cannon and a 105mm howitzer.

Next page
The bible of the Rangers. The pocket-sized Ranger Handbook *contains information on everything from combat orders to survival and first aid. A Ranger can refresh his memory on knots or explosives, or recall the use of map overlays or the different ways of laying an ambush. All the basics of Ranger training and operations are included. Issued in Ranger school, a Ranger keeps his handbook with him throughout his Ranger career.*

RANGER TRAINING BRIGADE
UNITED STATES ARMY INFANTRY SCHOOL
FORT BENNING, GEORGIA
June 1988

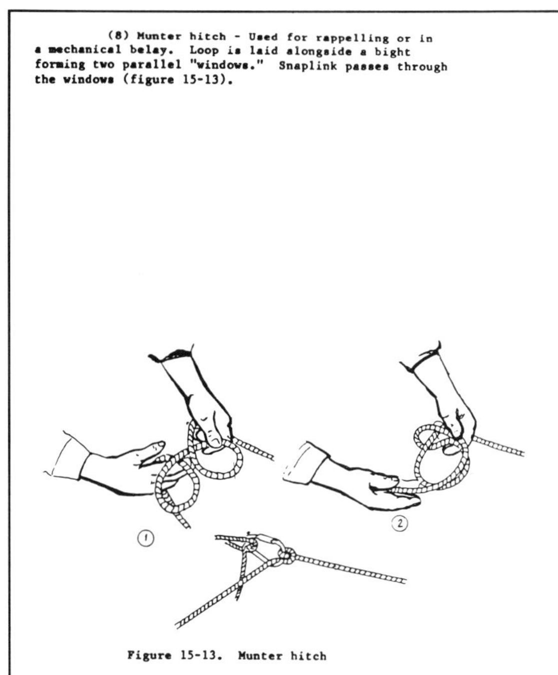

(8) Munter hitch - Used for rappelling or in a mechanical belay. Loop is laid alongside a bight forming two parallel "windows." Snaplink passes through the windows (figure 15-13).

Figure 15-13. Munter hitch

b. Other Ambush Formations. The V, X and Z are all variations of the basic linear and L formations. They are more advanced ambush formations and the leader <u>must</u> be an expert in the basics before he employs these more complicated ambush techniques.

(1) V formation (figure 5-16). The V-shape attack force elements are placed along both sides of the enemy route so that they form a V. Care must be taken to ensure that neither group (or leg) fires into the other. This formation subjects the enemy to both enfilading and interlocking fire. When employed in dense terrain, the legs of the V close in as the lead elements of the enemy force approach the point of the V. The legs then open fire at close range. Fire must be closely coordinated and controlled to ensure that the fires from one leg do not endanger the other leg. Wider separation of the elements makes this formation difficult to control, and there are fewer sites that favor its use. Its main advantage is that it is difficult for the enemy to detect the ambush until well into the kill zone.

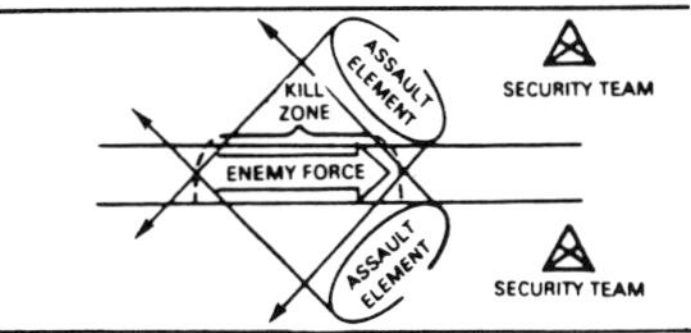

Figure 5-16. V-Ambush.

(2) <u>L-Shaped Ambush</u>. The L-shaped ambush is a variation of the linear ambush which employs flanking as well as infilade fires (figure 5-15). The short leg prevents escape or reinforcement. The L-ambush is formed with the base (bottom) of the L perpendicular to the expected enemy direction of advance. This is a good ambush for a road, trail, or any place where the ambush force can be sure of the enemy approach route. The L-ambush can handle an enemy coming from the expected direction (toward the base of the L) and from the front (stem of the L). It is less effective but usuable against an enemy formation that comes from the opposite direction than expected. In this case, the ambush must be executed when the enemy main body has cleared the base of the L. The flank security must protect the rear of the L base. In the L-ambush, weapons must be carefully sited to avoid direct or ricochet fire into friendly forces. Don't forget about the security elements when planning fire fans.

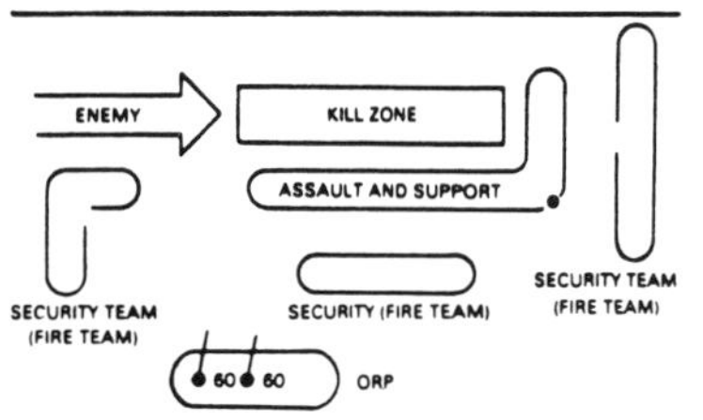

Figure 5-15. L-Shaped Ambush Formation.

Appendix

Ranger Milestones

Three milestones in Ranger history occurred in 1992.

The first was the fortieth anniverary of the Ranger school, which occurred on 20 March, when the Ranger Training Brigade graduated Class 4-92. Members of the first class to earn the Ranger tab, Class 1-52, attended the ceremonies. To commemorate the event, the brigade announced the establishment of the Ranger Hall of Fame to honor and preserve the contributions of the most extraordinary Rangers in American history. All those who served in a Ranger unit in combat, or who graduated from the US Army Ranger Training Course are eligible for membership. The brigade hopes to induct a substantial number of men from each era in Ranger history by 1997. Brigade headquarters at Fort Benning will house the Ranger Hall of Fame until a suitable facility is made available.

The second was the tenth anniversary of the Best Ranger Competition—a multiday event for two-man Ranger teams from throughout the US Army, Navy, and Marine Corps—which occurred from May 1 through 4, 1992. Participants in the competition, named for Lt. Gen. (Ret.) David E. Grange, Jr., must be airborne- and Ranger-qualified, on hazardous duty orders, have no adverse personnel record, and assigned to a unit receiving a formal invitation to compete. The winning teams receive pistols and the runners-up, knives. Sixty-four teams took part in 1992.

To provide funds for the Hall of Fame, and also for the annual Best Ranger Competition and the Ranger Store which sells such items as T-shirts, the brigade established the Ranger Association Fund, a nonprofit organization. The fund allows the Ranger Training Brigade to receive private and corporate donations to support these activities. Contributions may be sent care of The Ranger Training Brigade, Fort Benning, Georgia.

The third milestone was the fiftieth anniversary of the creation of Darby's Rangers, which occurred in June. The 75th Ranger Regiment and the World War II Ranger Battalions Association hosted a celebration June 17 through 20 at Fort Benning. Beginning with a regimental airborne operation on the morning of June 17, the four days were filled with competitions and reunions.

A special Ranger exhibit was set up in the National Infantry Museum, Fort Benning, as part of the fiftieth anniversary celebrations. Items on display include Maj. Gen. Frank D. Merrill's uniform and decorations, battle flags from various Ranger battalions, and special equipment such as the "knuckle-duster" knife invented by a member of the 1st Ranger Battalion. The exhibit will remain in the "Ranger Room" on the third floor of the National Infantry Museum until such time as a permanent Ranger wing is added to the museum. Maintenance of the Ranger Room and the proposed wing is supplemented by private donations.

As part of the fiftieth anniversay ceremonies, ground was broken for the Ranger Memorial in Ranger Field on Main Post at Fort Benning. The Memorial will include a tree-lined walk leading to monuments to all Ranger units. The site will eventually host various official and social functions. Fort Benning was chosen as the location for the memorial because it is the headquarters of the modern Rangers of the 75th Ranger Regiment and the site of the Ranger Training Brigade, where all Rangers receive their training. The location and planned monuments will provide a dignified memorial to the fallen and an inspiration to all Rangers and those who aspire to be Rangers. The memorial and walk are funded entirely by private contributions. Tax-deductible contributions may be sent to:

The Ranger Memorial Foundation, Inc.
c/o NCOA Service Center
2029 South Lumpkin Road
Columbus, GA 31903

The Ranger Regiment Association welcomes both present and former Rangers as full members. Non-Rangers may become associate members.

The Ranger Regiment Association

TO SPONSOR AN ASSOCIATION WHICH REPRESENTS RANGERS CURRENTLY ASSIGNED TO THE 75TH RANGER REGIMENT, AND THOSE WHO SERVED UNDER THE CHARTER OF GENERAL CREIGHTON ABRAMS, SINCE 1974

TO GAIN SUPPORT WITHIN THE CIVILIAN AND MILITARY COMMUNITIES

TO PROMOTE THE LINEAGE OF RANGERS AND TO SUPPORT THE INTEGRITY AND IDENTITY OF EACH EXISTING RANGER ASSOCIATION

TO SERVE ALL RANGER ASSOCIATIONS; TO REPRESENT, SPONSOR AND SAFEGUARD LINEAGE AND HERALDRY, AND SERVE AS THE CUSTODIAN FOR DONATED HISTORICAL/MUSEUM ITEMS

THE RANGER REGIMENT ASSOCIATION IS ESTABLISHED TO BRING TOGETHER THE BROTHERHOOD OF RANGERS AND PEOPLE WITH A COMMON INTEREST IN SUPPORTING RANGER ACTIVITIES

TO PROMOTE THE VALUES ESTABLISHED IN THE RANGER CREED, TO HONOR RANGERS, THEIR FAMILIES AND FRIENDS

TO ESTABLISH A RANGER TRUST FUND THAT PROVIDES MONETARY ASSISTANCE FOR THE FAMILIES OF FALLEN COMRADES

TO PROVIDE AN INSTITUTION FOR MANAGING REGIMENTAL FUNDS AND SPONSORING ACTIVITIES WHICH ACHIEVE THESE MEANS

RANGERS LEAD THE WAY!

Selected Sources

A standard source for the colonial period, which discusses Rangers, is Lawrence H. Gipson, *The British Empire Before the American Revolution*, particularly vol. 6, *The Years of Defeat* (New York: Alfred A. Knopf, 1946-1947). For Braddock's defeat, we recommend Paul E. Kopperman, *Braddock at the Monongahela* (Pittsburgh: University of Pittsburgh Press, 1976), which contains a bibliography and differs with Stanley Pargellis, "Braddock's Defeat," *American Historical Review* 41 (Jan. 1936), 253-269; the same author's *Military Affairs in North America, 1784-1765 . . .* (New York: D. Appleton-Century, 1936) has documents pertinent to a study of Rangers. That Braddock used Rangers is shown by Pargellis as well as by Franklin Thayer Nichols, "The Organization of Braddock's Army," *William & Mary Quarterly* 4 (April 1947), 125-147.

Indispensable for wilderness warfare, Rangers, and light infantry are Daniel J. Beattie, "The Adaptation of the British Army to Wilderness Warfare, 1755-1763," in Maarten Ultee, ed. *Adapting to Conditions* (Alabama: University of Alabama Press, 1986), 56-83, and Peter E. Russell, "Redcoats in the Wilderness: British Officers and Irregular Warfare in Europe and America, 1740 to 1760," *William & Mary Quarterly* 35 (1978), 629-652. Also useful are John K. Mahon, "Anglo-American Methods of Indian Warfare, 1676-1794," *Mississippi Valley Historical Review* 45 (1958), 244-275, and Edward Pierce Hamilton, "Colonial Warfare in North America," *Proceedings of Massachusetts Historical Society* 80 (1968), 3-15.

Burt B. Loescher's *The History of Rogers' Rangers: The Beginnings, 1755-1758*, published in California by the author, is not easily found. More generally available is John R. Cuneo, *Robert Rogers of the Rangers* (New York: Oxford University Press, 1959). These works were used to describe the attire and weapons of the Rangers. Rogers' *Journals of Major Robert Rogers* (New York: Corinth Books, 1961) describes their missions. Gary Zaboly has described "The Battle on Snowshoes," in *American History Illustrated* 14 (Dec. 1979), 122. Of interest and some curiosity is T. D. Seymour, editor, "A Ballad of Rogers' Rangers' Retreat, 1759," *Vermont History* 46 (Winter 1978), 21-23, detailing the disastrous retreat after the St. Francis raid.

George Washington's first Ranger unit is described by Sheldon Cohen, "The Death of Colonel Thomas Knowlton," *Connecticut Historical Society Bulletin* 30 (April 1965), 50-70. A. Theodore Steegman, Jr., "New York Rangers in the Hampshire Grants 1776-1777," *Vermont History* 51 (Fall 1983) 238-248, describes a rebel unit. For Tories, see Kenneth Scott, "Captain Christopher Benson's First Independent Company of New York Rangers 1777-1782," *National Genealogical Society Quarterly* 73 (June 1985), 132-134. Robert Rogers' attempt to set up British Rangers is detailed in John Cuneo, "The Early Days of the Queen's Rangers, August 1776-1777," *Military Affairs* 22 (Summer 1958), 65-74. Larry Ivers' short history, in manuscript form, of the Rangers covers aspects of the war in the north, and is available at the Donovan Technical Library, Fort Benning, Georgia.

For the south, see Jack Weller's "Irregular Warfare in the South," *Military Affairs* 24 (Fall 1960), 124-136, and "Irregular but Effective . . . ," *Military Affairs* 21 (Fall 1957), 118-136. For a detailed account of one organization, see Gary Olson, "Thomas Brown, Loyalist Partisan, and the Revolutionary War in Georgia 1777-1782," *Georgia Historical Quarterly* 54 (Nos. 1 and 2, 1970). Much the same ground is covered in W. Calvin Smith, "Mermaids Riding Alligators," *Florida Historical Quarterly* (April 1976), 443-464.

Francis Marion's military career is detailed in John Ferling, "Francis Marion," *Dictionary of American Military Biography* II (Westport, Conn.: Greenwood Press, 1984), 730-731; and George W. Kyte, "Francis Marion as Intelligence Officer," *South Carolina History Magazine* 77 (Oct. 1976), 215-226. A popular description is George J. Scheer, "The Elusive Swamp Fox," *American Heritage* 9 (April 1958), 41-47, 111.

Rangers continued to exist in the early national period, but information is sparse. Larry Ivers has written a short description of one unit in Florida in "Rangers in Florida—1818," *Infantry* (Sep.-Oct. 1963), 37. Otis E. Young has written "The United States Mounted Ranger Battalion, 1832-1833," *Mississippi Valley Historical Review* 41 (Dec. 1954), 453-470.

The rise and fall of Confederate Rangers is described by Carl E. Grant, "Partisan Warfare, Model 1861-65," *Military Review* 38 (Nov. 1958), 42-56. Andrew Brown's, "The First Mississippi Partisan Rangers," *Civil War History* 1 (Dec. 1955), 371-399, describes their activities and supports the view that such units were of little value to the Confederacy.

Grierson's raids are detailed in Edward Longacre, *Mounted Raids of the Civil War* (New York: A. S. Barnes), and Edwin Bearss, "Grierson's Winter Raid on the Mobile and Ohio Railroad," in *Military Analysis of the Civil War* (Millwood, N.Y.: American Military Institute, KTO Press, 1977).

Information on Darby and his Rangers may be found in Michael J. King, *William Orlando Darby: A Military Biography* (Hamden, Conn.: Archon Books, 1981), and from interviews with Darby before his death, *We Led The Way: Darby's Rangers* (San Rafael, Calif.: Presidio Press, 1980). James Altieri's pictorial history *Darby's Rangers* (Durham, N.C.: Seeman Printery, 1945), is hard to locate but worth the attempt, as is his *The Spearheaders* (New York: Bobbs-Merrill Co., 1960). The most recent, and in many ways the best, account of the Rangers at Cisterna appears in Carlo D'Este, *Fatal Decision* (New York: Harper Collins Publishers, 1991), chapter 10.

D-day and the Rangers can be studied in the war department's "Pointe Due Hoe (2nd Ranger Battalion, 6 June 1944)," part of the *Small Unit Actions* series published in 1946 and since reprinted. Short sketches of each Ranger unit may be found in James Ladd, *Commandos and Rangers of World War II* (New York: St. Martins Press, 1978). Michael King has written *Rangers: Selected Combat Operations in World War II*, Leavenworth Papers (No. 11, June 1985). King describes the prisoner of war raid in the Philippines, as well as Rangers in Africa, Sicily, and the Zerf operation in Europe.

Scott R. McMichael discusses the FSSF in *A Historical Perspective on Light Infantry* (Fort Leavenworth, Kan., US Army Command and General Staff College, 1987).

McMichael also discusses Merrill's Marauders, whose operations are traced in the Army Official Histories, such as Charles Romanus, *Stillwell's Command Problems* (Washington, D.C.: *Office of the Chief of Military History*, 1956), and in an Army monograph, *Merrill's Marauders Feb-May 1944*, published in 1945 and reissued in 1990. Controversy over the unit's treatment, especially by Stillwell's command, is highlighted in Charton Ogburn, Jr., *The Marauders* (New York: Harper & Bros., 1959), which describes the hunger and rituals surrounding meals. Following the war, the Army published "The Marauders: A Record of Righteous Indignation" in *Crisis Fleeting*, 293-396, compiled and edited by James H. Stone, which contains doctors' reports from the China-Burma-India theater. Published in 1969 by the Department of the Army, it in large measure supports McMichael. The debate is renewed in Scott McMichael, "Common Man, Uncommon Leadership: Colonel Charles N. Hunter with Galahad in

Burma," *Parameters* 16 (Summer 1986), 99-111. Several rejoinders appeared in a later issue of *Parameters* 17 (Spring 1987), 45-56. George McGee, Jr., has published *The History of the 2nd Battalion, Merrill's Marauders* (privately published, 1987); he is one of those who sharply disagrees with the doctors and McMichael.

For the Rangers during the Korea War, see Robert Black, *Rangers in Korea* (New York: Ballantine Books, 1989). Martin Blumenson has described a Ranger action in "The Rangers at Hwachon Dam," *Army* (Dec. 1967), 37-53.

Michael Lanning has a short history of the Rangers in his *Inside the LRRPs: Rangers in Vietnam* (New York: Ballantine Books, 1988), where he describes their missions and how the LRRPs became Rangers.

Ranger missions in Grenada are described in Mark Adkin, *Urgent Fury: The Battle for Grenada* (Lexington, Mass.: Lexington Books, 1987), which must be used with great caution. Rangers we interviewed who are knowledgeable about the Grenada action dispute some of Adkin's facts. Much information is still classified.

Some information on Rangers in Panama was found in Godfrey Harris, *Invasion: The American Destruction of the Noriega Regime in Panama* (Los Angeles, Calif.: The Americas Group, 1990).

Little or nothing is available on the Rangers in Desert Storm. One source is Ron Martz, "Behind the Line Teams Paid Off in Gulf War," *The Atlanta Journal/The Atlanta Constitution* Saturday October 19, 1991.

Index

Now from Motorbooks International, The POWER Series provides an in-depth look at the troops, weapon systems, ships, planes, machinery and missions of the world's modern military forces. From training to battle action, the top military units are detailed and illustrated with top quality color and black and white photography.

Available through book shops and specialty stores or direct. Call toll free 1-800-826-6600. From overseas 715-294-3345 or fax 715-294-4448

***AIRBORNE: Assault from the Sky*—**
by Hans Halberstadt
America's front line parachute divisions

***AIR GUARD: America's Flying Militia*—**
by George Hall
From the cockpit on their flying missions

***ARMY AVIATION*—**by Hans Halberstadt
American power house; how it evolved, how it works

***DESERT SHIELD: The Build-up; The Complete Story*—**by Robert F. Dorr
All the action leading up to Operation Desert Storm

***DESERT STORM AIR WAR*—**
by Robert F. Dorr
Blow-by-blow account of the allied air force and naval air campaign to liberate Kuwait

***DESERT STORM GROUND WAR*—**
by Hans Halberstadt
Soldier's-eye view of the allied ground victory over Iraq

***CV: Carrier Aviation*—**
by Peter Garrison and George Hall
Directly from the flight deck

***GREEN BERETS: Unconventional Warriors*—**by Hans Halberstadt
"To liberate from oppression"

***ISRAEL'S ARMY*—**by Samuel M. Katz
Inside this elite modern fighting force

ISRAEL'S AIR FORCE
by Samuel M. Katz
Inside the world's most combat-proven air force

***MARINE AIR: First to Fight*—**
by John Trotti and George Hall
America's most versatile assault force

***NTC: A Primer of Modern Mechanized Combat*—**by Hans Halberstadt
The US National (Tank and Helicopter) Training Center

***STRIKE: US Naval Strike Warfare Center*—**
by John Joss and George Hall
US Navy's "Top Gun" for ground attack pilots

***TANK ATTACK: A Primer of Modern Tank Warfare*—**
by Steven J. Zaloga and Michael Green
American tanks and tactics in the 1990s

***TOP GUN: The Navy's Fighter Weapons School*—**by George Hall
The best of the best

***USCG: Always Ready*—**by Hans Halberstadt
Coast Guard search and rescue, Alaska patrol and more

***SPACE SHUTTLE: The Quest Continues*—**
by George J. Torres
Pre-shuttle and shuttle operations history

More titles are constantly in preparation